LOST SOULS AND MAD SAINTS

Finding Faith in the Wilderness of Mental Illness

Orin Scandrett

May 3, 2005

LOST SOULS AND MAD SAINTS
By Orin Scandrett

Published by:

Sharing Press
Minneapolis, MN
612-827-2727

ISBN 0-9740954-1-9

BookSurge Publishing
An Amazon.com Company

CONTENTS

HEARING VOICES

An Introduction

At age seventeen, Joan of Arc heard a voice calling her to free France from English oppression. The army commanders thought she was crazy and laughed at her. Then they followed her as they liberated the besieged city of Orleans. Charles was crowned King of France as the Maid of Orleans stood by his side with sword and armor.

Joan insisted to the very end that her voices had come from God. But the court condemned her as a witch and burned her at the stake.

Today, she is remembered as a beloved and canonized saint.

Was Joan of Arc a lost soul or a mad saint? Did God speak to her from a distant heaven? Had the powers of evil seduced her? Or was she simply a delusional teenager suffering from an acute personality disorder?

External voices send thousands of vibrations to our eardrums each day. Parents, teachers, friends, leaders, TV and radio commercials, CDs, tapes, public address systems, cell phones, and our own larynxes all spew commands, instructions, warnings, facts, explanations, descriptions, and conclusions into the air. The bombardment of voices continues day after day, year after year, and decade after decade. Our sanity survives because we tune out some of the messages.

Meanwhile, a variety of internal voices direct, guide, warn, and inspire us in the multiple decisions and activities of life. Normal people participate in this form of mental imagery much of the time, and creative people do so more than most.

Authors and artists talk about their creative voices as gifts presented to the mind from some spontaneous source. Wolfgang Amadeus Mozart, the greatest composer of the classical period, frankly admitted, "Whence and how they come, I know not; nor can I force them." The sounds of compositions entered his thinking in their finished forms. "Some almighty power" spoke Nietzsche's creative masterpiece into his head as he walked beside a lake. Einstein compared the generation of a new idea to a chicken laying an egg. "Cheep—and all at once it is there."

In fact, all of us live by the voice of intuition—knowledge that comes to us without any conscious remembering or reasoning. We don't recall when or how it was learned, but we know it as true. It speaks from the storehouse of unconscious wisdom that has accumulated in the past but is used in the present. It tells us what to do in the hundreds of choices we make each day. We cannot function without this voice.

Yet sometimes our intuition is wrong.

When we refer to the voice of conscience, we place intuition in a moral context. We say, "this is wrong" or "that is right" even though we don't remember how or when we arrived at that conclusion. And we may (and often do) internally debate the merits of these moral reminders.

The psychologist Rollo May suggested that people cannot live without inner voices that generate and participate in a constant dialogue with new ideas.

When these voices come into conflict, the resulting paradox promotes growth, healing, and creativity.

This dynamic dialog of internal voices dramatically chatter within every person each day, and often continue during sleep. These conversations help us to live, move, and experience our lives sanely and fully.

Unless something goes wrong with the brain.

When the brain breaks, all life comes apart, and the internal voices turn into a mush of confusion. We call this a mental breakdown.

We define voices as psychotic when the person hearing them doesn't recognize that they exist only in the mind, and responds to them as if they are real.

The schizophrenic may use imaginary voices or other hallucinations to resolve the tension created by two contradictory commands that cannot be internally admitted or discussed. They break out of their dilemma into a psychotic world rather than face an internal conflict.

The person with a personality disorder escapes the unendurable pain of reality by creating a new identity and a different existence.

The delusional person struggles to determine which voice is real and ends up making the wrong decision.

All of this produces immense confusion in the mind of someone with a mental illness. And when psychiatrists and psychologists diagnose all internal voices—including loving, caring, supportive ones—as psychotic, this confusion multiplies like cancer.

Some philosophers and thinkers define all internal conversation as spiritual. If God dwells within the person, they tell us, then the divine speaks like any other inner voice.

Others insist that God exists (and must exist) in another dimension, outside of the body. If this is so, then how does God communicate? Does a supernatural voice enter the outer ear and vibrate through the skull? If so, is it audible? Can it be heard in the ear of someone standing close by?

The strict interpreter must say yes, but most believers would declare, "The spirit of God, though existing outside of the human form, joins the personality—spirit—in the faith experience." In this merger, God's voice speaks and is heard not as an external sound, but like all other internal voices.

How, then, is it possible to separate delusion from spirituality? How do we make such discernment? Is it possible to be mentally ill and, at the same time, hear the authentic voice of God? Or, perhaps more crucially, is it possible to be fully sane and hear the authentic voice of God?

Did Joan of Arc have a broken brain? Is that why the civil authorities diagnosed her as a lost soul and burned her at the stake? And, if mentally ill, was she capable of hearing the authentic voice of God? How did the canonizing investigators determine that Joan of Arc did hear God speak and was, indeed, a saint on an angry mission?

Lost Souls and Mad Saints is an attempt to explore these questions. At its heart is the conviction that people with serious and persistent mental illness can learn to discriminate between the authentic speaking of God and the delusional, confusing, and angry voices of a broken brain.

Twenty-two years ago, the voice of God invited me to get involved in the spiritual lives of mentally ill people living in the central city of Minneapolis. I entered a living laboratory in discovering how people with broken brains discern the voice of God and how humans, sane or insane, communicate with God.

All of the narratives in this volume are true. I personally observed, experienced, or listened to the story of each person. I have attempted to recreate each person's voice as authentically as possible. With a few deliberate exceptions I identified each one with their given names. (I have rarely used surnames in an attempt to provide some degree of confidentiality.)

I verified each voice with resources beyond my own memory. I secured verbal and written accounts from people who were still alive and locatable, and visited with relatives and friends of the deceased. In many cases I used recorded and written testimonials.

I authenticated the voice of my own personal story by drawing from daily journals, hospital and legal records, transcribed interviews, counseling notes, and the memories of relatives and friends.

I did exercise literary license in the area of chronology. The deliberate elimination of many year dates and some rearranging of the sequence of events allowed me to present incidents and developments within a single biographical account.

In every one of the true stories presented here, the authentic voice of God penetrated (at least temporarily) the fog of broken brains and the constant confusion of disturbed minds, because the people in question had internal ears that heard.

They listened with a desperate vulnerability. The darkness of their lostness generated a deep desire to embrace the sound waves flowing into their hearts and inner ears from God.

They listened with a determined silence. They learned to tune out the conflicting, clamoring, and distracting distortions, and to allow God's voice to infiltrate the isolated quietness.

They demonstrated that God actively speaks to us and the Divine voice can be heard when we are open and silent.

LOST SOULS AND MAD SAINTS

THE LOST

Hidden in the shadows of prestigious office buildings, glowing department store windows, warm hospitals, and ornate steeples, I found a group of invisible people. To call it a society ignored their isolation. Fraternity suggested a connection too personal. Culture denoted an association too organized. Still, these thousands of persons recognized each other as having a common existence, as populating the same neighborhoods and public places. This was the world of the mentally ill living in the city.

Embarrassment forged the connection. The shame projected upon and recognized by each person kept them hidden. Their public display of symptoms resulted in eviction and, sometimes, arrest.

The de-institutionalization program launched by the federal government had crashed, dumping these people into the central city of Minneapolis and creating a ghetto of human debris.

I sensed God speaking to me as I followed these persons through the frozen January streets of the inner city, searching for a spirituality that could be meaningful to them. The journey challenged my theology, religious training, ordination vows, and personal beliefs.

It began when the police department recognized that the average cop lacked the training needed to deal with the snake-pit issues of the mentally ill. The chief asked the county to provide a psychiatric emergency room.

Dr. Zigfried Stelmacher heard the need, received the approval of the county board, and organized a crisis intervention center. It operated as part of the emergency room at the old Minneapolis General Hospital. Pastors responded to Stelmacher's call by volunteering to answer phones and consult with persons experiencing mental trauma. I spent Thursdays, midnight to eight a.m., at the center before leaving on my weekend trips to visit churches and pastors across the five state area, as Conference Superintendent.

The difference between these callers and the patients I met in the hospital startled me. Persons with a faith history who suffered in the intensive care, cardiac, surgical, and burn units would include prayer as part of their healing processes. Even those with a generally indifferent attitude toward religion would find faith important in times of crisis. In stark contrast, the individuals diagnosed as seriously and persistently mentally ill seemed spiritually alone—separated from God.

The open admission of lostness shared by many persons with major mental illness presented a refreshing and even inspiring vulnerability. They understood, at the outset, the New Testament Greek meaning of "confession"—to acknowledge and concede a need.

Hennepin County Social Services and Church Women United pooled their resources to develop a community support center known as The Circle F. The center leadership responded enthusiastically to my idea of organizing a Spiritual Life Group—a meeting where these lost and shunned people could share in a mutual search for answers.

The interest and attendance grew, but it only intensified and magnified the dilemma. Worship, prayer, and Bible study with one another in a warm and healthy environment met desperate physical and social needs, but it did little to help the participants deal with their separation from God.

I discovered that persons with clinical depression often felt abandoned by God. Women and men with schizophrenia, mania, and other delusional disorders experienced psychosis in the form of religious voices, powers, and fears, leaving them unable to trust the voice of God, their own intuitions, and personal conscience. Every day, I met people who heard voices telling them to commit suicide, murder, and sexual assault. "God's" voice told them to do terrible things that led to their hospitalization, arrest, and incarceration. Their confusion intensified when they believed that God and religion caused their illness.

My program director discovered a unique and profound emphasis in Minneapolis psychotics. He observed that while the delusions of people in Washington, D.C. fixated on political figures and mentally ill Californians obsessed over the rich and famous, the Minnesota disturbed mind tended to focus on religion. His conclusion: encourage patients to eliminate religious thoughts and actions. The message my group members heard: "God made you sick."

I understood the confusion at a deeper level when I became the chaplain in Andrew Care Home, the newly-constructed warehouse for two hundred and forty mentally ill clients, and observed the services provided for them by the different churches and synagogues of the community.

Some religions blamed the victims by viewing all emotional problems as the direct result of personal sin and bad choices.

One afternoon I listened to Richard, a schizophrenic pianist, perform the William Tell Overture. When done, he turned from the keyboard, faced me and blurted, "Pastor, do you think I'm going to hell?"

I asked, "Why do you think you might go to hell?"

He responded, "Remember, David Helfgott got sick because he didn't play the piano like his Jewish father wanted. I know God made me schizophrenic because I couldn't play like my Jewish mama wanted." Such ideas separated many people like Richard from God.

In the theology of some churches, evil powers emerged as the cause of mental disease.

A pastor called early one Saturday morning. "Barb has come to our home in a spiritual crisis. She asked me to call you. Could you come over?" When I arrived, he pulled me through the door and pointed to a plastic receptacle on the living room carpet.

"We're ready," he whispered.

"Ready for what?"

"For the putrid green bile she'll expel when we exorcize her. I know how it works."

Barb was cowering in the corner. I moved toward her.

The pastor grabbed me. In my face he shouted, "So you don't believe the Bible? What kind of a Christian are you?"

"Have you called an ambulance?" I asked.

He shook his head.

"What do you do when someone has a heart attack, a diabetic seizure, a fractured arm? You call the paramedics, right? Why do you refuse hospital help for a broken brain?"

The idea of demon possession survives in Minneapolis. I visited one worship service where the speaker placed his hands on the head of a mentally ill man and repeatedly screamed, "heal!" The only sane response in the entire chapel came from a traumatized six-year old, who exclaimed through his tears, "Mama, I want to go home."

A more destructive idea proclaimed mental illness as ordered by God's deliberate will. "God's plan for the world includes a certain number of paranoid schizophrenics, and you are one of them." Yet even the diseased mind could not excuse God for causing such undeserved pain.

One Thursday night I received a call from a building manager. He had seen John, one of my mentally ill friends, running naked through the halls and across the front yard. I eventually coaxed John back into his apartment.

There, I found certificates from social service agencies verifying that John had completed many different training programs for independent living. At each graduation the young man had reached the place where he could function well, maintain an apartment, and work at a part-time job. Then, he would stop taking medication and crash. Each time, John's pastor had told him, "If you truly believe in God and want to be a real Christian, you will flush away your drugs and trust the Holy Spirit."

A fundamentalist pastor dogmatically declared in his preaching, "God sends mental disorders as a divine punishment for terrible sin." Such theology demanded confessions from diseased persons. He forced his mentally ill listeners to search for the hidden evil inside themselves.

Most mentally ill persons had the intelligence and awareness to recognize such attitudes as prejudiced and patronizing. They responded appropriately, with seething resentment and distrust.

Eventually the Andrew Care Home management dealt with the confusion by banning all in-house worship services.

Mental disorders stem from organic and physical abnormalities. Environmental stresses often trigger genetic factors, but the fundamental causes emerge from a wide variety of breaks in the brain. In the world of the seriously and persistently mentally ill (SPMI), all "fix-it" therapy theories have been tried and discarded as failures. It doesn't matter how good these persons might feel this day, this week, this month, this year; they never can be entirely well.

How can a viable spiritual life exist in the midst of continual confusion and social isolation? Can someone be mentally ill and spiritually whole?

In January 1980, while obsessed with these questions, I attended a metro-wide church growth conference. As I heard Bob Maxwell, a nationally-known growth expert, present his enthusiastic vision of a successful mega-church, I felt pulled by the twin emotions of anger and compassion generated by the paradox of Christmas in the central city. The luxurious shop windows glowing with wealth, the warmth and smells of fine restaurants, the laughter and camaraderie of office parties, and the huge, warm, and vacant night spaces all sneered at the trudging, SSI-dependent, hungry, freezing, and isolated citizens of the inner city. They lived in a world excluded from the wealthy, homey, and peaceful image of Christmas projected by the media, society, and the church. The season epitomized the trashing of humanity that affected the poor, the lonely, the hospitalized, and, especially, those with mental illness.

As Maxwell spoke, I heard the voice of God drowning out his words. "Would you leave your church office and become a full-time pastor with the homeless, handicapped, and mentally ill persons in the inner city of Minneapolis?"

My soul screamed, "Yes!"

I walked out of the meeting, went home, talked with my wife, and wrote a letter of resignation.

Bishop Van Valin requested that I meet him in Kansas City to discuss my decision. In our meeting, he heard the cry of my heart and agreed that I must choose between the leadership call of the church and my inner conviction from God. I officially resigned on the third day of May, my fiftieth birthday.

Shari, the manager of the Fair Oaks Motel on the corner of Twenty-fourth Street and Third Avenue, in inner-city Minneapolis, responded to my passion and excitement. She volunteered to provide the lower-level dining room of the restaurant for Sunday meetings.

I invited residents from the seventeen Board and Care homes in the neighborhood. The first invitations read: "FAIR OAKS CHRISTIAN FELLOWSHIP. Join with us for spiritual fellowship and a free breakfast." My simple and naïve vision: a place and a time to share our lostness and begin the spiritual search together.

A phone call came from the dining room manager late Saturday night. Someone had showed him a card describing the opening meeting and the free breakfast.

"Pastor," he said, "do you know that in this neighborhood a free meal on Sunday morning will attract hundreds of hungry residents? We agreed to provide food for thirty people, not the entire neighborhood."

After discussion, he consented to keep the plan if I would call the police for crowd control when he ran out of food.

Eighteen persons enjoyed breakfast together that first Sunday morning.

Larry started the group sharing by telling his personal story. He mumbled words through his protecting hands, clasped in front of his face. His head remained bowed. His eyes never made contact with anyone.

"To be honest, I came because of the food. I was hungry for a real breakfast.

"I stay in the old Andrews Hotel. I've lived there since moving from Dallas about two years ago. Each month I get a General Assistance payment of $125.00. One-third goes to pay for my room. Hennepin County pays the rest of my rent.

"I moved to Minneapolis because it's much easier to obtain social security disability here in Minnesota than in Texas. Also, I wanted to get away from my mother and an ex-girlfriend.

"My father abandoned us. I don't remember him. My mother took care of me. She scrubbed floors in nursing homes to put me through Southern Methodist University. I completed my undergraduate degree, started studying for my master's at Perkins School of Religion, and planned to be married to a wonderful woman.

"Then I had my break.

"While I was sick, I tried to kill my mother and started running with gay friends. I became very paranoid of women. Mother told me I couldn't stay at home anymore. She couldn't deal with it. I lost my job at a bookstore and have been living in shelters the past three years.

"I guess that's my story. Oh, my mother belongs to the Unitarian Church, but I became a Christian while attending Southern. Thirty percent of the student body listed Methodist as a church preference. So I joined the campus church and enrolled in studies to become a pastor.

"I don't know what I believe. I refuse to attend church anymore."

Melanie attended that first meeting. She simply announced, "I found the flyer telling about Fair Oaks Fellowship saying that a pastor was meeting with people who were having emotional problems. It gave me hope. I thought, 'I don't have anything to lose,' and came."

After the discussion had continued for more than an hour, a painfully thin young man in his twenties began to speak. He deliberately forced each word, syllable by syllable, from his lips. I waited for him to slowly complete his first sentence and wondered how long it would take for him to tell us what he wanted us to hear. He paused, rocked back and forth in his chair as if trying to create momentum, and then continued.

"I'm Paul. This is Janet. We've been married three months and five days. We met at New Horizons. They taught us how to live on our own. They told us we could get an apartment and live together. I belonged to the Episcopalian Church and that is where we got married. I work at a job for handicapped people at Honeywell. I assemble books and papers in the printing department. Janet works at Goodwill.

"I'm confused about this religious stuff. I had a seizure and called Love Lines. The Christian counselor told me I could be delivered from the demons. He told me to find a church that believed in the Holy Spirit. I talked to my priest. He told me that I'm already filled with God's spirit. I want to talk with a pastor or someone who understands people with problems like mine."

I responded, "Paul, the purpose for this time together is to share our spiritual problems. Could we meet sometime this week and talk more about your confusion?"

He nodded an assent and continued. "Phyllis lives in our building. I told her about this meeting and she wanted to come with us. She and her little baby need help."

I had met Phyllis when she came in the door. She looked no more than fifteen years old. The tiny baby had stayed motionless in the little canvas folding stroller while her mother ate breakfast. Phyllis looked up from her plate with fear-filled eyes.

"I came to ask for prayer for Lisa and me. I'm hearing those voices again. I don't think right anymore. I can't remember when it's time for Lisa's bottle. I'm afraid someone might hurt my little girl. I think I need to talk to my doctor, but if I go to the hospital, they'll take my baby away."

I turned toward Phyllis. "Don't you think you need to take Lisa and go to the Crisis Center? They'll help you with your medications and be sure no one hurts your little girl. Would it be okay if we all prayed together for you and your little baby, and then I went with you to the hospital?"

She nodded her head in silent agreement.

We closed the meeting by joining hands in a circle of silent prayer.

THE MAD

Watching a person fight for sanity, lose their grip on it, struggle to grab it back, and finally let go presents an awesome and frightening spectacle.

I remember entering the old City Hall at midnight and riding the elevator to Hennepin County Jail. The detention supervisor asked me to provide bail money and take custody of Allen. His aggressive demands for release had escalated, creating a management problem. The psychiatric nurse recommended the dismissal of charges. She had located Allen's parents in Palm Springs, but they refused involvement.

Allen's erratic driving had alerted the police. They attempted to escort him to the Crisis Center. Allen agreed to go, but didn't want to leave his girlfriend alone on the street. Allen became enraged when the police refused to take her home. In the confrontation, two policemen threw Allen's head against the curb, broke his glasses, blackened his eyes, bruised his face, and detained him for assaulting an officer.

Angry feelings surfaced as I drove Allen home and helped him clean his injured face. What had happened to this beloved son of devoutly Jewish parents? Born into a wealthy highly respected family of Minneapolis business leaders, and raised with the best in a mansion listed in the national historic records, he had functioned for three years as a sophisticated, educated, and trained executive in one of the many family companies.

He traveled the world and spent a month each summer cruising the Caribbean. An old picture in Allen's wallet showed him happily waving from the red leather seat of a cream-colored Chrysler convertible.

That night he walked in a Haldol shuffle, his body bloated by medications. He lived in a filthy subsidized apartment on the limited funds of social security disability. Once each year the embarrassed family made contact and invited him to join them in a private winter cruise. Alienated from relatives and friends, and aggressive toward any social contacts, he lived the confusing and hopeless daily trauma of a paranoid schizophrenic.

Angry phone calls, as many as ten a day, followed. Allen demanded that I listen to his endless tirades. If I refused to answer he would leave messages until the machine ran out of tape. "You can't hang up on me. Pastors don't hang up on people." "If you hang up the phone I'll call you back every minute until you talk to me." "My father has abandoned me." "I'm forbidden to visit my old office." "The Jewish religion and God did this to me." "The violence in the Torah frightens me." "All doctors, especially psychiatrists, are ignorant." "Medications are poison." "I saw some blacks shopping at Byerly's in St. Louis Park. When did we start allowing blacks in our neighborhood?" "I went to the mayor's office today but he wouldn't see me." "I keep phoning the governor but he won't return my calls."

I invited Allen to meet with me each Thursday for noon breakfast at the Chef's Café on Franklin. (His heavy dosage of psychotropic meds kept him from functioning until late in the day. He routinely fell asleep at dawn for a few hours of fitful rest.) Typically, Allen started his abusive yelling as he entered the café door and kept it going until I walked out on him an hour later. It became routine for the manager to announce, "If you can't keep your voice down, you'll have to leave." Allen never allowed me to pick up the tab.

I listened to Allen's tirades of anger and hate for weeks, then months. He blamed his father, his father's religion, Jewish culture, and God for his problems.

When Allen became schizophrenic at age twenty-four, his father had refused to let him continue as an executive in one of his companies, forced him to apply for social security disability, set up a trust fund that provided a credit card and $1000 a month, and moved him out of their home into an assisted living apartment. Allen rehearsed, daily, the things he would scream at deceased Papa, if he would ever resurrect from the dead.

Convinced that the Jewish religion and culture had forced Papa to abandon him, and determined to get even, Allen built grand fantasies of how to destroy rabbis, synagogues, and Israel. Today, he would have been arrested, for hundreds of people heard his terroristic threats.

Once, I facetiously asked him, "Would you like to destroy God, too?" His surprising answer was, "No, but I'd like to destroy anybody who is stupid enough to do His will." He condemned the Torah and the Hebrew Bible because "it tells about a God that destroyed wholesale any person and nation opposing Israel and murdered Hebrews who didn't do His will." Allen claimed to be an atheist, but how could he blame a God that didn't exist?

Allen's paranoid mind saw the behavior of others as the cause of his problems. He believed he could be well if people would start treating him fairly. His actions caused more rejection, especially from those in authority.

I soon discovered that Allen's ranting was harmless. He desperately needed someone to hear and authenticate the frustration and rage flowing from his powerlessness and loneliness. I felt the pain as I watched him lose control of life.

Disintegration takes on a spiritual dimension when the trauma of mental illness destroys trust in God, intuition, and conscience. As people lose their world-views, value systems and moral guides, radical changes in personality and behavior not directly related to the diseases can appear.

Spiritual lostness often begins when persons recognize that they have a serious and persistent mental illness. Sometimes it happens during the first major episode, especially when their behavior is frightening and dangerous. Other individuals deny their condition for months or years; as they recover from each episode they convince themselves that, at last, they have returned to normal.

Eventually, a particularly horrific experience awakens an inner awareness of a serious, debilitating, and chronic problem. (Crisis therapists diagnose such moments of insight as potentially dangerous and, sometimes, lethal.)

When people let go of God in the face of trauma, they become much more than persons not right with God. They are impoverished by the loss of a series of vital spiritual attributes that are essential to living a full life. Their confused world-view disrupts their long held value constructs. In a religious person, the foundation of their moral structure rests on God. When a mental illness interferes with their belief system, it changes their core. It forces them to assess themselves as having no value. As they realize that their disease has taken away everything important—vocation, money, success, marriage, sex, family, home, the enjoyment of relationships, and common respect, the trauma of worthlessness further traumatizes the trauma.

Ruth approached me after our Christmas fellowship celebration in her usual brusque manner. "I have something to show you and I want you to do a favor for me."

She unwrapped a life-sized oil portrait of her daughter that an artist had painted from a high school graduation photo. The expensive frame made the beautiful young girl look regal. "Will you take this gift to my daughter for Christmas?"

I didn't need to ask, "Why me?" or "Why not take it yourself?" I understood the pain in her question.

For more than twenty-five years Ruth had worked as a waitress in the five-star hotels of Chicago. As a single parent, she raised her son Kyle and daughter Bernadette, bought a nice house, and stashed a little money in a savings account. When she was 24, Bernadette discovered a restaurant for sale in the warehouse district of Minneapolis. She convinced her mother to sell the home in Chicago and move to the Twin Cities. They could afford the down payment on both the café and a house by pooling their assets. The plan: Ruth would care for her two-year-old granddaughter, Nicole, and Bernadette would manage the business.

But Ruth became unexpectedly agitated and violent as she entered menopause. A suicide threat resulted in a seventy-two hour hold, the diagnosis of major depressive disorder, and admission to a psychiatric unit.

Bernadette refused to let her mother return home after she was discharged from the hospital. She feared for the safety of the granddaughter. Enraged, Ruth repeatedly tried to force her way into her own house. Bernadette petitioned for and obtained a legal order for protection. The court prevented Ruth from having any contact with little Nicole.

Ruth lived ten years without any communication with Bernadette, Nicole, or other family members. She hid in the hallway outside the café a few times, hoping to catch a glimpse of the daughter and granddaughter that she loved with all of her heart.

Ruth existed on a $350-a month social security disability allowance. One third went to pay for a third-floor walk up apartment. The lack of money caused her little concern. She survived. But the rejection of family fed her anger and despair.

When agitated, Ruth could become horrific and frightful. Neighbors in the Chicago Avenue Apartments and patrons of Danny's Bar gave her a wide berth. She had few friends.

Ruth resented the Lutheran Church. "It baptized, confirmed, and rejected me. It teaches a religion of guilt and punishment."

She professed the teachings of the Baha`i faith. "They accept people from every religious background." "If there is a God, He's way off somewhere and has nothing to do with me."

I delivered the unwrapped portrait to Bernadette. I handed it to her as she stood in a petite holiday apron behind the lunch counter. She announced to everyone in the room, "This is the ghost from my Christmas past." To me she said, "Tell her I never, never, never want to see her again."

It made the anger boil in my own soul.

Eventually a tsunami of hopelessness washed away all of Ruth's wanting and wishing. A disorder of willing emerged as her dreams disappeared. Many disturbed men and women like Ruth reached the heartrending stalemate of being afraid to even want. Expectations saddled them with heavy loads of fearful and painful disappointments.

Larry's sharing at the Fair Oaks Fellowship did not prepare me for the cowering person I met at the Andrews Hotel coffee shop. He entered the room with his chin forced down against the chest, eyes fixed on the floor, hands folded across his face as if to ward off some type of blow, and the butt of a cigarette protruding through tar-stained fingers.

He greeted me by slowly bending his shoulders and bowing his baldhead like an oriental coolie. His eyes displayed the wary fear of an abused animal. A timid gentle voice spoke four words: "You want to talk?"

I don't recall my exact response, but I indicated an interest in the theological position of the Perkins school. It opened his beautiful mind.

He enlightened me regarding the practical theology of pastoral care created by James Fowler in clarifying and reworking the structuralism of

Jean Piaget, the psychology of Erik Erikson, and the faith phenomenologies of Niebuhr and Tillich.

He wondered if I might be familiar with Paul Tournier and his attempts to put the insights of psychology and psychiatry into a Christian perspective. He excitedly described the community of Henri Nouwen and the L'Arche Network, where the mentally handicapped and their assistants live together as God's children, trying to flesh out the gospel.

That afternoon I discovered that this sophisticated and articulate soul reveled in philosophy, theology, and psychology. He quoted the classics to me, reviewed the current best sellers, and compared their authors eloquently.

I ended the session when my mind refused to digest any more inspiration from his animated face, and my lungs rebelled against the fumes from his chain-smoking. He apologized for both the stimulating thoughts that he had to vent somewhere and the addiction that demanded nicotine every hour of the night and day.

I begged his forgiveness for being a member of a society that dared to take an intellect like his, one that could grace the faculty of a university, and consign it to hibernation in a roach-invested flophouse.

Our mutual hug that morning began a growing bond of respect.

BECOMING LOST

A U-haul truck transported John from the sunshine of Kentucky to the cold reality of the inner city and a Minnesota winter. Fresh with the inspiration of God's call and the Holy Spirit's passion for ministry, he followed me into the frozen streets to face a world of spiritual chaos.

I bonded quickly with John, his lovely young wife Julie, and their two beautiful children. I seemed to re-live my first years as a pastor through him. Like me, he had been raised exclusively in the church culture and felt called by God to work with people who lived in society's shadows.

John grew up in Winona Lake, Indiana, an old camp-meeting town of 400 and the location of our world church headquarters. His father eventually resigned from his job as a church executive and moved to Wilmore, Kentucky, a little college town of 2000. There he accepted the chair of the Religious Education Department at Asbury Theological Seminary. John moved with dad and obtained his master's degree from the same institution.

Besides his internship in the inner city, John was director of the Douglas Chapel youth ministries on Minneapolis's north side. There the spaghetti of a new freeway system had isolated an old United Methodist Church building. The congregation left the area following the riots of 1968, and the District Board decided to make the old sanctuary a community center for hundreds of kids from the drug-infested neighborhood.

In both parts of his job, John felt that he had met all the powers of evil head on. I saw what kept him going: the assurance of a divine call and the daily inspiration of God's voice.

It happened on a cold Saturday morning. Julie called me, sobbing for help. She had spent most of the night trying to keep John from running, jumping, and roaming around the house and neighborhood.

I entered John's study to see him crouched on top of the desk, ready to leap into the air. "I'm going to fly. I could jump off the church tower and it wouldn't hurt me. I'm God."

He did leap onto the floor. He rolled over, dropped his pants, and writhed like a female animal in heat. "Rape me, rape me, God wants you to rape me."

An hour later I watched John pacing the Crisis Center holding room, waiting for an injection of Haldol in preparation for admission to the eighth floor of Hennepin County Medical Center.

How could it be? Could John end up like Larry, huddled in an eight-by-ten room, struggling to find pleasure in another cigarette? Could I?

"I think I'm beginning to believe in God again. I've been praying. Would you come and pray with me?"

The request came from a middle-aged woman named Trudy whom I had met some months earlier. She had called the crisis number requesting something to eat. When I pushed open the unlocked door of the apartment, I saw a one-armed creature huddled in a corner cave she had constructed from a dirty card table and the drapes torn from the window. The stench from a pile of bursting garbage bags filled the otherwise empty room.

I coaxed Trudy into going with me to the hospital. She cooperated. "I can trust you. You're a pastor." The way she spoke "pastor" convinced me that, at one time, church had been important in her life.

She had not seen her husband in seven years. He left her after she used a shotgun to blow off her arm in a suicide attempt.

Trudy had lived alone in that bare apartment since her discharge, two years earlier, from Willmar State Hospital. With no follow-up and little medication, Trudy's mental health had deteriorated daily.

I helped Trudy get stabilized at the hospital and, after her discharge, social services arranged for her admission to Oak Grove Care Home.

This day, though, Trudy needed spiritual sustenance. She met me at the door of Oak Grove bundled in a long down coat. "Pastor, I know it's cold, but the sun looks bright and warm. Could we go for a walk?"

We walked and talked our way around the lake in Loring Park. I prayed. She prayed. As I escorted her up the steps to Oak Grove, I thought, "This is what being a pastor is all about."

Trudy disappeared that night. The note found on the bedside stand simply said, "Thank you and the pastor for this nice day. Tell the pastor, I did what God told me to do." Her down coat hung on the back of the door and the snow boots stood neatly in the hall.

They found her two days later. Her frozen body clad in a filmy negligee, lay curled in a sleeping position. Trudy had crawled into the bushes along Parade Stadium and deliberately frozen to death.

A few days later I received an angry letter written by her enraged son. "Why didn't you stop her? You killed her...you and that useless nurse. You let her freeze to death. You let her crawl into those bushes and die like an old dog."

Judy had come to our house on an irregular basis for months. At age 29 she had been living with chronic schizophrenia for seven years. She got along quite well with psychiatric care, heavy medication, and the faithful support of her husband.

A psychiatrist had referred Judy to me because of her strong church background and her obsessive thoughts about religion.

The request for counseling this night came as no surprise. Judy's husband, a Ramsey County park employee, had flown to California to fight forest fires. Before he left, he had advised, "Judy might call you for counseling if she becomes frightened of being alone and has suicidal thoughts."

When I opened the door, Judy walked by me without saying a word. She went to the couch, sat down, and closed her eyes. After several minutes of silence, she announced, "I'm such a bad person. I don't deserve to live."

"What makes you feel like bad person?" I asked.

"The voice keeps saying, 'Judy, you are a bad, bad girl.'"

"What voice? Who is talking to you?"

"The same voice, the voice of my Dad. I told you before. If I did something my Dad thought was wrong, he would stand me in the middle of the kitchen table, demand that I look at him, and say, 'Does Judy know she is a bad, bad girl? Does Judy know that we can't let bad little girls live in our house? Judy, you are bad, bad little girl.'"

"Did something happen, Judy? What makes you feel worse today?"

"Roger phoned me this afternoon. He had worked the line last night and couldn't call earlier. I asked him to come home. He told me he didn't know when they would be back. I got mad. I told him, 'I can't stand it. When you get here you'll find me dead.' He told me to call you."

"Judy, did you have any thoughts of killing yourself before Roger called? How did things go at the agency today?"

Judy began to relax as she described her trip to Mankato with the Environmental Protection Agency. They had selected her from the other volunteers to make the trip and collect air samples.

"Judy, are you having any suicidal thoughts right now?"

She responded, "No, not now, but I'm not going home tonight." She rolled off the couch and slumped, face down, on the floor. "Judy, what's wrong? Are you sick? Do we need to call a doctor?"

She refused to respond.

Finally, I announced, "Judy, you can't stay here tonight. If you're afraid to go home, I'll need to call the paramedics and put you in the hospital."

Donna joined me in helping Judy into a chair. Judy pleaded, "I can't drive, I'm too upset. Will you take home?"

I said, "Sure, I'll take you home."

Judy responded by suddenly screaming, "No, I can't be home alone without a car. You drive me home in my car."

I agreed, and told Donna I would call her if I couldn't catch a bus back home.

After ten-minutes of pleading, persuading, and pushing, Judy made it into the car and we started for her home.

We rode in complete silence until we turned off I-94 on Lexington and neared her street. Suddenly, she opened the passenger door and lunged toward it like she planned to jump. I commanded, "Stop it. Get that door shut." She refused.

I pulled to the curb, reached over for the door, pulled it shut, and punched the lock. During the last six blocks to her house I drove with one hand holding her door shut.

As I helped Judy into her house, I said, "I need to call your doctor. He may want to put you in the hospital. I'm afraid to leave you in this condition."

She disappeared into the bedroom. I sat down on the couch, picked up the phone, and dialed.

The next moment, I saw Judy's naked body in the doorway. She ran across the room, jumped on my lap, threw her arms around my neck, and pressed her breasts into my face. "God told me we should have sex together. He wants me to make love to you."

I yelled, "Get your clothes on right now or I'm calling 911." I pushed her onto the floor, leaped up, fled to the bathroom, and locked the door.

I stood for minutes resting my head against the mirror, trying to keep my body from shaking.

After a short and agonizing wait, a remorseful, apologetic, and fully dressed Judy invited me to open the door and use the phone. I did reach Dr. Cramer. He consoled me and assessed Judy. I called Donna, asked her to pick me up, and made my retreat.

I walked over to Como Park. I had told Donna I would meet her by the fountain. As I sat waiting in the dark, I dared to face the question I had heard so many times in fellowship sharing: "Is there really a God, and does he really meet and speak with us?"

An inner voice told young Brad to cut off his finger with a hatchet.

He explained to me, "The next thing I remember, I was being wheeled in a chair into a locked room. Well, anyway, I sensed this entity...this voice...he was there. He said, 'I thought you would like it this way.'

"I was lying down in one of the rooms and all of a sudden this...voice said, 'You did wrong to my daughter.' He said, 'Look at me, look at me.' He was so angry with me! The doctor said, 'Who are you looking at?' I looked over at him several times. That was when my mother first thought I was schizophrenic, when she saw that.

"There was this one day that...the voice made me laugh at these jokes. I sensed him and I heard him. I didn't see him...

"The voice showed me death. I was very nervous. I went to the cemetery and I thought about all the souls that couldn't get out. It scared me. I had the sensation I was dead and people were shoveling dirt over me. I felt like I was dead for a million years. I was worried about death...

"The voice told me to cut off my finger, and I did. I bought an axe and did it. The man at the store didn't like blood all over the place, so I left and went to my mother's house."

I thought back to the day I wrote my letter of resignation to the Bishop. Those once-theoretical questions had become traumatically personal. How could I have a viable spiritual life in the midst of this madness and confusion? Did God ever speak to me? Was God's voice, the voice that had spoken to me so clearly and convincingly, the flashing synapses of my own deluded mind? Because I had heard the voice of God speaking directly to me, was I mentally ill?

The county medical examiner called me to the morgue to consult with a Native American grandmother. "We need your help over here."

I remember the light in the examining room: a smoky aura filtered indirectly from some far off source. I recall the muffled throb of the ventilator fans. I pushed through to the chrome table and lifted the sheet.

I hesitated, waiting for the chill to spread across my skin and for the lightness to enter my brain. Through the mist, I studied the tiny, crumpled form. No serene sleeping doll here.

The boy's head looked grotesque and huge attached to a little bloody chunk of person. One small curled hand appeared to be grasping for a finger. I put mine there and swallowed the gasp that the touch aroused in me.

I could not ignore the two arrows protruding from the bloated stomach. I felt the adrenaline of rage rush into my arms. Who would do such a thing, and why?

A closer look enabled me to conclude that someone had driven the arrows through the child's ribs and into the heart. The lack of bleeding made it clear even to my untrained mind that the child had died prior to the mutilation.

I withdrew my hand and turned away. The medical examainer understood, pulled the sheet over little Bubas, and escorted me to the holding room.

Cora, the grandmother, huddled in a corner with her face pressed against the wall. I touched her shoulder and she turned toward me. I looked for signs of guilt and remorse, but found none. Her terror-filled eyes looked directly into mine as she spoke. "He was a child of the devil, and nothing will ever change my mind."

"Did you kill Bubas, Cora?"

"I pushed the pillow down over Bubas' face, but he wouldn't die. The evil made him strong."

"How did it happen?"

"We were playing out in the field when it came to me what I had to do. I knew I'd rather have my grandson dead than possessed by the devil."

"Can you tell me why you did it, Cora?"

"I had to fight for him. He was my grandson. I got to my apartment and realized right away what I had to do. I couldn't stop. I wanted to make him sleep as painless as possible. I had to deliver him from evil."

"Cora, I need to know. Tell me. Why did you use the sticks?"

"I used them to drive out and kill that spirit—that devil. The Sun Dance stakes are powerful."

Cora was clearly oriented to the time and the place. She had no psychosis—no hallucinations. Her settled conviction that the Creator had chosen her to save her grandchild fit the diagnosis of a fixed delusion.

I faced one simple question: was she a danger to herself and others?

My answer: "She killed a twenty-month-old child." I signed the emergency hold. The doctors on Psych would decide her sanity.

On my own crisis day, the police had called. They had found Danny kneeling in prayer with his face on a Bible and a gun in hand. His suicide note explained that our reading the Bible and praying together had convinced him that God demanded his own death. The police asked me to meet them at his apartment.

Afterward, I made my own way from that gruesome scene to the Hennepin County Crisis Center. I didn't want to live any longer. I couldn't face one more day. Moving any muscle demanded a concentrated effort. My mind refused to focus. I felt so scared.

I knew every counselor in the center. We had worked many midnight shifts together. But on that day they looked and moved like fearful monsters.

Vicki watched me come in the door. She sensed my pain, grasped me by the hand, and led me into a conference room. The shaking refused to stop. Neither of us said anything. I sunk to my knees. She rolled her chair to my side and took me in her arms. I tried to tell her about Danny, but the sobs choked the words.

I don't know how long she held me. It seemed like ages. Then I was in a chair trying to explain the call from the police and Danny's death.

The next few hours passed as a blur, but my intake chart reads: "Client is tearful and shaking after collapsing in this counselor's arms. Intermittently calmed with holding and extended conversation.

"Articulate. Oriented x3. Depressed mood with agitation. Flat affect. No psychotic or delusional symptoms. Memory intact. Responds coherently to questions. Pressured speech with compulsive weeping. Reports insomnia, agitation, fatigue, diminished ability to think, and feelings of worthlessness. No suicidal thinking, but has recurrent thoughts of wanting to die.

"Impression: Axis I ... 296.23 Major Depressive Episode. V62.82 Bereavement. R/O 309.81 Post Traumatic Stress Disorder.

"Plan: 1) Refer to Psychiatry for out-patient TX. 2) Contact Director of Chaplain Services to arrange referral to Psychiatry. 3) Return to CIC, PRN."

They referred me to Psychiatry with a diagnosis of Clinical Depression.

BECOMING MAD

I couldn't trust God anymore. I tried to exercise faith, but God wouldn't (or couldn't) deliver me from evil. I knew God didn't live in me. A note I wrote in my prayer journal reads: "God, I want to love you with all of my heart, mind, soul and strength, but I don't know how. Help me. Help me. Show me the way."

I felt I couldn't exist any longer. I didn't want to live without the awareness of the God I had known since fourteen years of age.

Ken, my therapist, opened our fourth session with a leading question. "We agreed to explore your spiritual journey today. The referral from CIC views your primary condition as clinical, but suggests that religious concerns precipitated your depressive episode. Last session we both concluded that you brought this on yourself. In a sense you needed to experience despair. Well, where do we begin?"

"Where do I begin? I think it started in January, 1980 when God called me to resign from the church office and become an inner-city pastor. God asked me to spend all of my time working with mentally handicapped people."

Ken interrupted, "What do you mean, God asked you?"

"He asked me. He spoke to me. The voice of God asked me, 'Would you leave your church office and become a full-time pastor with the mentally ill persons of Minneapolis?' The words were so clear that I went home and wrote a letter of resignation to my bishop."

Ken smiled, lifted his eyebrows in surprise, and asked, "Are you saying that you hear voices from God speaking to you personally?"

"Sometimes… not often, but sometimes, yes…"

Ken swiveled in his chair, faced me, and pressed further. "What do you mean when you speak of experiencing God? Describe it to me."

"Well, it's an inner voice."

"An audible voce?" he asked in an incredulous and patronizing tone.

Waves of humiliation flushed through me. "Yes, sometimes, but more often I would describe it as an awareness, a consciousness of the presence of God. It's very real. It has existed with me for years…but…now…that spiritual feeling is gone. Today I'm isolated and separated from God."

"It came with the depression?" Ken asked in an eager tone.

"I don't know. It's difficult to describe. The presence seems suspended. The lack of it makes me break into sobbing, and I feel like I don't want to live any longer."

"We've talked about those feelings before. Later we'll need to take a deeper look, but right now I want you to explain the experiences where God seems to speak to you. I don't understand. Enlighten me."

I looked at him. I could see in his face that he thought—no, knew—I was delusional. We were living in two different galaxies.

"The real issue has surfaced," I told him. "I can't ignore it. You asked the question. I gave you my answer."

"So the voices telling your counselees to kill themselves were delusional, but the voices you hear in your own head are authentic?"

"Well, I guess...I feel...I think..." my words became a whisper as I groped for an answer. "I know, that's the question. Did Danny hear God telling him to commit suicide? I don't think so. I hope not. But I know God's voice has spoken to me."

"Are you trying to convince me of that?"

"No, I don't think I can convince you. I guess I'm trying to persuade myself." I paused, searching for the right words. "Let me tell you about one of my God experiences. It was 1960. I was 30 years old. I don't know why, but the Board of Bishops invited me to be one of the keynote speakers at the Centennial World General Conference of my church. I spent two months praying about that speech, searching for a message from God. If someone would have asked me if I received inspiration from God, I would have said, 'Yes, I meditated, prayed, and have a settled conviction of the words I should say.'

"But I was scared. On the drive down to Indiana, Donna and the boys asked me what my deep sighs were about. I remember trying to explain the fears and my feelings of inadequacy.

"Dr. Northup met me at the front of the auditorium. He told me, 'I'll return in about an hour, escort you to the pulpit, and do the introduction.' I remember seeing his huge back and his impressive dark pinstripe suit, and then looking down at my little light gray thirty dollar Penney's suit. I began fighting a rush of feelings in my chest.

"I remember opening the side door and walking down the stairs into an open room. I went to a table, pulled out a chair, sat down, opened my folder, and started looking over the words of my speech.

"Then I felt a new surge of emotions. I told myself, 'Pull yourself together now. Don't let things get out of hand.'

"Suddenly, I sensed a warm light surrounding my body. It looked to me like a translucent, shoulder high fog.

"Then, waves and waves of presence that I felt as love washed over me. It seemed to flow through every cell of my mind and each tissue of my body.

"I remember thinking, 'Why, it's God...it's God's love!'

"The sensation was so strong I could barely walk.

"I know that Dr. Northup came and found me standing in the middle of the lower-level room. I must have followed him up the stairs to the sanctuary. He didn't seem to notice anything unusual in my behavior, and I entered the pulpit on cue.

"At that moment, God's voice began speaking through my mind and mouth. The words seemed to come from between the crowd of people and me.

"It was a powerful voice, but it sounded gentle and loving. The words seemed to go on forever. Finally, I sat down.

"Silence followed. It seemed endless, but probably lasted no more than two minutes.

"Then, people were standing, kneeling, weeping, and pressing forward to the front of the auditorium.

"I stood there and told myself, 'I will never speak in my own voice again.' But, of course, I did."

I looked into Ken's face. "That voice was as real as our conversation in this session today. No, it was more real. And many other people in that auditorium heard the words. Are you telling me that the whole experience was just the psychotic whisperings of a confused mind?

"What's your honest diagnosis? Psychotic? A delusional disorder? The Grandiose Type? Mixed? Unspecified? What would you list on Axis I and Axis II?"

Ken gave me another patronizing smile. "You know, that's only your depression talking."

"You didn't answer my question. Was that experience a delusion? Do you think I'm delusional? I know you've done a mental status exam. What are your conclusions?"

The nonchalance left his face. He said soberly, "Of course those are delusions. You're a crisis counselor and you know the meaning of delusional. I don't see you as psychotic—but delusional? Yes."

I started to stand up, then caught myself and relaxed back into the chair. "Ken, I base my whole life on talking with God and experiencing God. If people who talk with God are deluded, what does that say about the 74 percent of Americans who say they believe in a Divine Being and pray to God? Your position presupposes a secular view of normal, and rules all religions as insane. If I'm mentally ill because I hear the voice of God, then isn't anyone who prays, anyone who believes in God and searches for God's will, mentally ill as well?"

I couldn't stop. "In a democratic society that claims to protect religious freedom, how can you assume that some people's beliefs are legitimate and commendable, but my relationship with God is insane? Do you define all religion as delusional?"

Ken didn't argue. He looked like he wanted to reach out and give my head a sympathetic pat, as if he were comforting a child burning with fever. He said, "The DSM-III states that 'false beliefs' by definition are delusions. I believe you do have spiritual problems. It must be difficult for someone like you to lose faith in God. But, hearing voices, having God speak through you, and receiving commands from fantasy beings... I see those as grandiose. I think the most devout Christian in your church would agree."

I stood up. "Every United States Senate session begins with a prayer led by the chaplain. Does that make them delusional? Or do they simply keep their fingers crossed behind their backs until the Amen?"

"Come on now, let's be reasonable."

"Ken, you and I both know people in our community, and in this hospital, who share many irrational ideas, but that doesn't mean they have schizophrenic, depressed, broken brains."

The words continued to pour from my mouth. "I had a college Bible professor who believed the Earth came into existence in exactly six days, six thousand years ago. He scoffed at geological evidence proving the world to be millions of years old. He may have been deceived, or foolish, but few psychiatrists in the world would diagnose him as crazy."

Ken stood, grasped my shoulder in his hand, and looked into my face. He asked, "Orin, are you ready to let go of your sick obsession with God?"

Suddenly I understood the jarring pain of the denial, disapproval, and condescension inflicted upon the mentally ill by psychiatric professionals.

At the same time, I felt my God disappearing into a dark whirlpool of fear and doubt.

"Ken, I don't know what to think anymore. I meet with people every day who have heard voices from God telling them to commit suicide, kill other people, have sex with me, and engage in destructive behaviors. God's voice tells them to do terrible things.

"And if I confessed to my supervisor or my co-workers that God spoke to me, like I just told you, they would label me as psychotic.

"You're telling me that the voice of God exists as a creation of my own disturbed mind. The spiritual voices and my years of believing have no meaning. To you, it's all depression and a mood."

I suddenly realized I was shouting.

My feelings of humiliation had turned into rage. I was losing God, religious culture, sacred language, and spiritual meaning. A door was opening to loneliness, fatigue, and despair.

I tottered on the edge of that chasm of total darkness—the world of lost souls and mad saints.

BECOMING FOUND

I terminated therapy.

That week I struggled to explain my pain and anger in a phone call to my son Tim. He had already fled the city and what he called the "insanity of civilization" by walking away from a scholarship at Chicago Theological Seminary, hitchhiking to Big Sur, California, and disappearing into the Los Padres National Forest. Tim knew the power of seclusion and believed in the wilderness.

He told me, "Dad, leave the city and live, here, in nature. It will take care of the depression."

I bought a $250 round-trip plane ticket to San Francisco and an army surplus pup tent, sleeping bag, and cook kit at Harris Warehouse. I took off to stay 29 days, mostly alone, in the Ventanna Wilderness. My only previous camping experience: a weekend excursion with Donna's university friends that ended abruptly when borrowed, flimsy equipment failed to compete with three inches of snow.

One week later, embarrassed and filled with trepidation, I stepped off the Greyhound shuttle to Big Sur and into Tim's arms.

I wanted Tim to go with me, but I knew he wouldn't. He believed in the power of solitude. He did provide me with a Forest Service permit, a map of the river trail, and directions to Sike's Hot Springs.

I set off climbing the switchback trail leading out of the Pfeiffer-Big Sur valley and into the Sierra Salinas Mountains.

I started hearing voices the first night. At 1:30 a.m. somebody outside my tent screamed, "Get the snake! Get the snake! Don't let him get away! Get him, get him, get him!"

I got out of my sleeping bag, put on my boots, and climbed outside.

Total quiet. No one.

I went back in the tent and tried to sleep. The voices reappeared and became louder and angrier. They kept describing some kind of dangerous creature. I heard the words, clear and very loud. I got up two more times. Each time, outside the tent, I found myself completely alone.

I couldn't sleep. I prayed, "Is this a warning? Am I losing my mind? Help me."

Most nights, after that, the voices came from the river. Distinct words: "die, die, die" and "kill." Once a crying voice called, "come, come and come." I got up and stood at the water's edge; the voices disappeared. But, then, as I tried to sleep, they cried out again, and again, and again. Eventually, I learned that my tears made them stop. But when I quit crying, back they came.

A woman's laughing and singing awakened me one morning. Strange songs. At the time I understood the words. I tried to write them down, but I couldn't remember.

I crawled over to the river's edge.

Walking along the sand was a beautiful woman: nude, with long hair and a graceful body. She skipped in a sort of dance.

No lyrics this time...sounds, but more like a musical instrument—a singing with no distinct words. She followed the edge of the water and disappeared around the bend. She kept looking back at me, laughing at me, teasing me. She was seductive, but not in a sexual way.

I crossed the river and searched for her. No footprints, no campfire. No trace. I couldn't get that woman out of my mind.

I wanted to find her. I searched for her each morning at sunrise, but she never appeared again.

One day I walked across the river and started climbing the cliff up to the hot springs. I wanted to soak in the warm water. As I grabbed a little tree, it pulled out by the roots and I fell about fifteen feet. I turned a complete somersault and landed on my butt, hard, on a little ledge above the river rocks. I was fine except for a bruised finger. But my body began trembling, then shaking.

I was alone in the middle of the wilderness. If I broke a leg, who would know?

I dreaded dusk. Each approach of darkness spawned a black fear. The word "melancholy" emerged from my lips, again and again. I pleaded, "God be with me," but I didn't feel His presence anymore.

I filled the hours each morning by praying and reading the New Testament.

After a few days, a compulsion to write possessed me. It started out as journaling...but the memories accelerated until I scribbled for hours every day. I recorded page after page of flowing consciousness. I remembered things that seemed raw and fresh to my awareness. A tightly-wound internal tape seemed to play with increasing volume and velocity.

Anger and guilt surfaced. Their loudest expressions fixated on my mother. I mentioned her on many of the pages.

Then, suddenly, the memories stopped. Written out! I sat on the rocks and stared into the river.

Tim hiked in to check on me. It took him a while to find my camp. I had moved across the river and further downstream. He walked up to me as I cried, prayed, paced, and yelled at God.

It was a wonderful shock to see him standing there. He opened his backpack and poured out a pile of green pea pods. How delicious, after days of instant oatmeal and rice.

We talked. I told him what I had seen and heard.

Tim explained, "Quite often, people hear voices when out here, alone."

"Do they come from the spirit world, or are they delusions?" I asked him.

He didn't know.

He reminded me of the promise he had made on the phone. "Dad, if you spend a month out here, you'll find your answer." He urged me to stay in the wilderness the remaining days.

The next morning he told me, "I'll see you on the third," and headed out.

I felt a rush of love. "What a wonderful son! My beloved son."

April 29. I waited alone in the wilderness.

As darkness started to spread into the canyon that night, the deep black mood uncoiled inside my brain. The rays of the setting sun blazed across the mountain peak. As the light dropped, the shadows started crawling up the cliff toward the sky.

A voice (Inner? Audible? I'm not sure. Who cares?), began to sing softly, an old Sunday school song.

> Climb, climb up Sunshine Mountain, heavenly breezes blow.
> Climb, climb up Sunshine Mountain, faces all aglow.
> Turn, turn your eyes from evil, look up to the sky.
> Climb, climb up Sunshine Mountain, You and I.

Something inside my mind separated.

I sang the song over and over and over. I changed the time...I added rhythm...I sprung into dancing. I filled the approaching darkness with ecstatic energy.

I sang a prayer. "I want to climb, climb up Sunshine Mountain...I want to turn, turn my eyes from evil. I have a choice. I can turn from darkness...look up to the sky. Yes, God and I."

Then God spoke to me. "Orin, how about you and I climbing out of this darkness and living in the sunshine of My love?" Were they sounds or mental stimulation? I didn't know. But the words echoed. And I recognized the voice of God.

God pulsated beside me. I simply needed to turn and absorb His healing power of love.

I turned. I absorbed. I felt the love flow in.

I walked in light all that night. I couldn't sleep. I didn't try to sleep. I didn't want to sleep. I paced along the bank of the river exclaiming, "I see it. I see it."

I stopped viewing my clinical depression as a spiritual problem.

I understood. I knew I could be mentally ill and spiritually whole at the same time. I saw the difference between the voice of God and the voice of a broken brain.

I held the sacred answer in my soul, in my mind, in my hand.

I shouted into the empty wilderness air, "Thank you, God, for this new insight—this revelation."

I walked the river sand all night. New thoughts percolated. I tried to hold them in my mind. My frustration: the darkness prevented me from writing.

The next morning the bright sun seemed to illuminate each simple truth. Seated on a rock in the middle of nowhere, I wrote what God had discerned for me:

1) Psychotic and delusional voices sound angry. God's voice flows as love.

2) Psychotic and delusional voices make demands, treating persons as robots, giving orders. God's gentle, respectful, and suggestive voice treats the listener as a fellow being, and invites reciprocation.

3) Psychotic and delusional voices feel destructive, manipulative, and immoral. God's voice speaks in moral, supportive, and positive tones.

4) Psychotic and delusional voices suggest crazy things that don't make sense. God's voice sensibly respects the laws of nature and human nature.

5) Psychotic and delusional voices flaunt scripture. God's voice complements the Word of God.

6) Psychotic and delusional voices tend to rant and rave repeating the same commands over and over, like rock lyrics. God's voice makes clear and concise statements.

7) Psychotic and delusional voices move in circles. God's voice moves in a definite direction.

I stopped viewing my clinical depression as a spiritual problem. And I understood that even mentally ill persons had the power, and the ability, to discern the difference between the voice of God and the voices of a broken brain.

I understood what William James, the Harvard psychologist and his Varieties of Religious Experience, meant when he reported that religious people of all faiths experienced God as an awareness of "waves and waves of liquid love."

Thomas Aquinas expressed it succinctly: "When we are in God and God is in us, we love and we are love, perfectly, flawlessly, in the everlasting intimacy of friendship."

Two spirits—God and human—are intimately joined together. God continues as totally God and the human being remains completely human—partners in a relational dance, totally aware of each personality and responding together, in the pure music of love.

Love fuels the power of discernment.

I returned home. The wandering and wondering disappeared into love and understanding. The new light dispelled the darkness.

On my first day back with my family, I held my beautiful seven-month-old granddaughter in my arms as I sang, "Climb, climb up Sunshine Mountain." The bright sunlight reflected from her smiling face, and mine.

I awoke at five each morning, eager to spend two hours meditating in the presence of God, preparing for the unfolding of a new mission.

SEARCHING SOULS

I first met Don in a hospital room. He was a thin, frail, 34-year-old with a dual diagnosis of mental illness and chemical dependency. We developed a close relationship during his eleven weeks in the medical center.

Intoxicated Don had stumbled in front of a speeding car while walking home from a New Year's party. The accident smashed his head and face, put out an eye, and left him legally blind.

After three days in the hospital, he made a new commitment to sobriety. He maintained it for about five months. During that time he hosted a Spiritual Fellowship Group in the Cedar-Riverside Housing Complex.

Don complained to me after one Sunday meeting, "These people are so beautiful and I'm so ugly. I'll never fit in with a group like that. They'll never accept me."

While I was in the wilderness, Don cashed his $70 assistance check and spent it all on vodka.

In a drunken stupor, he set his apartment on fire. The rescue squad took him to Detox in an ambulance. The court committed Don to a three-week chemical dependency treatment program.

Don called me from the Hennepin County Treatment Center. Discharged from the program and recovering from smoke-damaged lungs, he needed transportation to his home.

I drove Don from Eighteenth and Chicago to Cedar-Riverside and wheeled him into McKnight Towers. We rode the elevator to the twenty-first floor.

I still cringe from the sight that met my eyes when we opened the door of his apartment.

Human excrement and vomit covered the rooms. Rotten food coated the kitchen counter. The stench made me physically sick.

I spent two hours mopping, scrubbing, and cleaning just to get him into the bedroom.

Disappointment, hurt, and anger burned in my heart. What was I doing here? What was the point? This person didn't care about himself or God. What a waste of time and energy!

In that moment of struggling pain, God met me.

The ceiling opened and Heaven appeared. In the vision, Donna and I stood, hand in hand, with Don and before God.

Don looked at me with a beautiful smile. His battered face appeared whole. The blind eye could see. His body glowed with health. He was transformed—a new body, a new soul, and a new mind.

God's voice echoed through the room: "Be confident of this, that He who began a good work in you will carry it on to completion." I recognized the words of promise from Philippians, chapter one, verse six.

A new beginning beckoned.

I affirmed a trust and hope that the One who made us would in due season disclose the gifts of restored relationships and renewed spirituality.

And, gradually, it began to happen.

In our Spiritual Fellowship Groups, lost souls from many religious backgrounds—Christianity, Judaism, Islam, Baha`i, Scientology, and other "isms" began to glow with spiritual life in ways that none of us could interpret or explain. Yet, in these groups over the next few months, the healing process evolved into a loose program.

We became conscious of four general phases: explaining God's love, exposing God's love, experiencing God's love, and exploring God's love. Sometimes the individual's spiritual formation followed definite linear stages, like a meal served in four courses. More often, people allowed the different emphases to percolate into a blended spiritual brew.

The phase of explaining God's love introduced a focus. I presented the purpose and process of the groups through one-on-one screening sessions with each seeker.

Understanding began with two simple truths: 1) A diseased and dysfunctional brain causes severe and persistent mental illness. God does not cause it. Evil and sin do not cause it. 2) God's voice can be discerned and separated from the hallucinations and delusions of the seriously and persistently mentally ill.

I invited participants to tell their religious and spiritual stories. My emphasis differed from the empathetic listening of a therapist. I attempted to restrict the ventilation to feelings about God, religion, and spirituality. Depending on the mental disorganization and mood of the ill person, this could take many brief meetings over a period of weeks. The searcher needed to sense that their spiritual disintegration and the resulting emotional pain had been heard and understood.

Following the ventilation experience, I wanted each person to comprehend what had happened to their relationships with God during their struggle with mental illness. They needed to recognize for themselves the "why" of their lostness. Their own story-telling exposed the reasons for their spiritual aloneness.

Sometime and somewhere in this sharing, the concept of God surfaced. At that point I attempted to guide the person in isolating, defining, and clarifying their ideas about God, and in separating God from their diseased condition. The critical agenda was to help the person rescind their myths about God, recognize that God did not cause their disease, and comprehend God's nature as unconditional love.

When people began to understand God's nature as love, everything seemed to change. This understanding acted as a new filter in their viewing and dealing with experiences and events. It reframed their concepts of self and opened the door to a more friendly and warm environment.

I advised each new seeker that the Spiritual Life Group consisted of people with similar stories and an ability to understand God at a much deeper level. The groups provided a safe place where participants could freely share questions, anger, fears, and guilt.

Their views of God did not change quickly or easily. The dynamics of the group, itself, proved more effective than any teaching or counseling. Group members traveled this path together, and together they discovered new spiritual life.

SOULS IN FELLOWSHIP

Donna and I arrive about thirty minutes early. Nevertheless Lorelie, Allen, Denise, and Sallie already wait in the banquet room foyer. A server unlocks the door and ushers us toward the two large urns of hot coffee and platters of cookies provided by the sympathetic dining room management.

Vickie, Melanie, Don, Larry, Shari, Jim, Zella, Jason, Molly, Alvie and Louise, Karline, Mark, James, Sue, Richard, Lars, Whitey, Chris, Ruth, Ernest, and some people I do not recognize filter into the room, get some coffee, and take seats around the circle of tables.

Larry is the group leader, one of five group members who have completed twelve months of study and group leadership training. He joins me at the end table and asks the group, "Does anyone have a special song you would like us to sing together?"

Several hands are raised. Ron, the operator of the tape player, begins jotting down the requests:

"Could we sing 'The Rose', by Bette Midler?"

"I want to sing 'Blowin' In the Wind.'

"I'd Like To Teach the World to Sing." "You've Got a Friend." "You Needed Me." "He Makes All Things Beautiful in His Time." "I Will Serve you Because I Love You." "Bring My Body Closer."

The tapes of these songs are played for thirty minutes and people sing along. I see tears slide down Melanie's cheek as she mouths the words: "I was nothing, until you found me...heartaches, broken people, ruined lives...Your touch is what I long for, you have given life to me."

After the last song has been sung, Larry announces, "Zella has a new song she wants to sing for us. Following Zella's song, we'll start around the circle and let each one share. If any one of you doesn't feel like talking today, simply say, 'I pass.' Please don't interrupt. Save your input and response until the person has finished speaking.

"Go ahead, Zella."

Zella sings:

"He's my Lord
And the Lord is in me
Praise the Lord
The Lord is in me
He's on my side
And the Lord is in me
He watches over me
He's my Lord
And the Lord is in me
Praise the Lord
The Lord is in me
I love him so
And the Lord is in me
He's the one to know"

Melanie, a petite brunette with a Boston accent, speaks. "I had feelings while we were singing. I've felt unloved from the first memories of my life. My parents called me a worthless person and said, 'Nobody wants you!' The most hurting thing: Four guys raped me. I ran to mom...scared, screaming, and bleeding. All she could say was, 'I hope you die.' Another time my mom took a butcher knife and threw it at me. I kept searching so hard for love. It ended in a nightmare.

"The man I loved committed suicide. We also had a little girl. Her name was Judy Lynn. I loved her very much. I still do. After she died, I just fell apart and spent several months in the hospital.

"Then I found some people who really loved me. I felt God really did love me. His love began to heal the deep pain of my life. I know how to love and forgive because God's Spirit lives in me."

Ruth, an older, heavy, gray haired woman, responds to Melanie through pursed lips. "I have the opposite problem. My daughter and granddaughter won't even let me come in their home. They refuse to speak to me. My daughter claims I abused her. I did hurt her, but I tried to follow what God told me. That's why I don't believe Melanie when she talks about God loving her.

"I believe there is a God, the power of the universe, way off somewhere, but he doesn't help me. It's the love of people that healed Melanie...not the love of God.

"My sister in Iowa writes me these letters. She tells me God can't help me because I haven't confessed my sins and repented. She thinks I'm going to hell. If God is love, then I have a lot more of God in me than she does in her. That's for sure."

James, a slender, muscular, and tanned twenty-eight year old, speaks next.

"Ruth talks about God telling her to hurt her daughter. Strange things started happening to me and I believed they were from God. My brother called the police and had me thrown out of the house because I pulled a knife and tried to kill him. A voice told me, 'Blow your brains out. I can't see you waste yourself like this.'

"I was afraid of God. I prayed once for my best friend. He shot himself. I prayed for my girlfriend. She died. I prayed that when I found my real father, he would love me as his son. When I found him, he was stoned and didn't want me around. I ended up with no place to stay.

"Then Ira found me and brought me to the fellowship. Week after week you told me, 'God loves us.'

"Then my brother had a terrible accident. He was in a coma for three months. I bowed my head by the hospital bed and prayed. As I prayed...God gave me a vision...a mental picture of my brother eating oranges. I jumped up, ran to the supermarket, bought some oranges, peeled one, and offered it to my brother. He ate it. Three days later he was sitting up...eating fruit by himself. Then I knew there was a God and He cared about me. Bad voices don't come from God."

Chris, an underweight and unkempt twenty-three year old kid with uncut blond hair and a scraggly beard, looks up and starts to weep. "God is telling me to kill myself right now. I keep saying, 'No, No, No!' He keeps telling me to walk in front of a bus. I yell 'Help me!' but people just look at me like they're afraid of me. Even with the meds I can't make the voice stop. I don't want to end up in the hospital again."

Shari, an attractive middle-aged mother, looks at Chris, breaks into tears, and softly says, "They took my son away from me seven years ago. I thought God told me not to feed him because of poison in the baby food. I didn't know the difference between God's speaking and the voices in my head. You know, with me, if it sounds like more than one voice or lots of voices and they're yelling at me...acting mean to me...mad at me, I just remember that God doesn't talk that way. God gives me one clear thought—soft and kind.

"Still, sometimes I can't ignore the noise of the voices. When they start to wear me out, I go talk to my counselor or ask my doctor for more meds. I know what it feels like to have voices screaming over and over, but I know God doesn't come to me that way."

For the next few minutes everyone is silent. Then, Larry says, "Let's hear from some of the rest of you. What has happened to you spiritually this week? Ron, how have things been going with you?"

Ron, a blond and energetic young Swede, hesitates, coughs into his hand and looks up. "I'm awful! I don't have any place to sleep. Our Saviors' Shelter won't allow drugs and that includes my meds. I can't go back there tonight. Does anyone know somewhere I can sleep?"

Larry responds, "You can sleep in the basement of my bookstore. John has a cot there now. There's room for another one."

Ron asks Larry, "You have a bookstore?"

"It's over on Lyndale and Twenty-second," Larry says. "The fellowship helped me start it after my eviction from the Andrews Hotel. See me afterward and I'll tell you more. Right now we should keep focused on spiritual needs. Do you wish to share today?"

"Yes, I do want to share. I've fallen in love. I brought my beautiful new friend with me. I've never been in love like this before and I want all of you to meet her. Molly, do you want to talk?"

A small young girl with long black hair jumps to her feet. She is dressed in a black leotard and a flowing red satin skirt. "Don't call me

Molly. Call me Gypsy Girl…my new name. Last year, when I turned eighteen, I ran away from my home in Cambridge, Minnesota to become a gypsy. I came to Minneapolis looking for a clan. I plan to start a group of my own if I can't find one. I read palms and I have the gift of telling fortunes. I charge twenty dollars an hour. Ron and I want to find an apartment with a storefront office for me. He plays the guitar and sings. I dance. Ron has agreed to change his name to Jason Light; I'm now called Gypsy Girl. We plan to form a song and dance team.

"Ron wanted me to come with him today. I worship Satan, like a good gypsy. I didn't think I'd like the fellowship, but when I heard you singing 'The Rose' God spoke to me. I feel a lot of love here. That's all I have to say." She sits back down.

Larry nods toward Karline and asks, "Karline, how has your week been?"

An elegantly dressed and well-coifed woman forces a smile and begins speaking, "Some of you know my problem. I have no emotional feelings. It's like I'm in a walking coma. I don't get angry. I can't feel sad. I never feel happy. When I went to the hospital the last time, my husband and two daughters agreed that I shouldn't come back home because they couldn't be with me every minute telling me when my choices were good or bad. I have no sense of difference between right and wrong. I can't feel God's presence, like you people do.

"William asked me to move in with him. He stays with me every minute. I need his direction in choosing food, taking a bath, and dressing. He brings me here, sits me in a chair, and picks me up when we're done.

Well, as you know, William has cancer and is dying. What happens to me when I lose him? Pray for me."

Larry promises, "We'll pray with you during our prayer time. We want to be with you during this crisis." He turns to Gloria. "Gloria, you've been praising the Lord the past two weeks. Is life still great for you?"

Gloria leans forward, radiating energy. "God is still walking with me. He's the living God who filled the need of my aching heart. He's the third god in my life.

"My first god was alcohol. My mother died when I was eight years old. Nobody cared what happened to me. I lived on the streets of Minneapolis until age sixteen, when I became a ward of the state. I spent the next eight years in institutions. The welfare office placed me in an independent living program for the handicapped. I started drinking to help me cope with life on my own. I became an alcoholic.

"Then I got into A A. It saved me. It kept me sober. It became my church and my god, but it didn't take away the loneliness of my heart. I still felt unloved and unwanted.

"Now I know the real God. I want to tell you all, again, that God lives in my heart. I pray that each of you in this group will come to know God in the same way. God loves me. God loves you. Ask God to enter your life."

"Alvie and Louise, do you two have anything to report this morning?" Larry asks.

Louise, a short and very plump woman with a young, soft face, looks at Alvie. Alvie shakes his head. She clears her throat and says, "I guess Alvie doesn't want to say anything. I want to bring you up to date on our on-going problem. The staff at Andrew residence continues to get mad at

Alvie for spending the whole day with me in my room and in the lounge. I tell them that I want him to come. I love him. He's my lover. Maggie, my social worker, can't understand how a woman of twenty-six can love a man who's eighty. She says, 'He's just using you.' I told her, 'How do you know I'm not using him?' She got mad and said, 'It's not healthy.' I had her there. I told her, 'I'm in Andrew and Alvie is in the nursing home because we're both certified by the state as unhealthy.' I feel God wants us to be together. We each were alone without God and now we have each other and God. I wish we could get married. Would you consider marrying us, Pastor?"

Larry says, "You might want to save that and talk to the pastor after our meeting. Whitey, you raised your hand. Do you have something to tell us?"

Whitey's albino hand brushes back his pure white hair. "I found a warm place to live for the winter. Ron, you could spend a night with me. They're building a new Mobil station on Third Avenue and Franklin. The construction company enclosed the whole area with plastic and installed a space heater. The crew works eight hours a day. I know how to get inside and I have the whole place to myself the rest of the time. I call that an answer to my prayer. And I don't need General Assistance any longer. My business of buying old bikes to fix up and sell provides all the money I need.

"I still forget sometimes and talk out loud to the voices in my head. If the police see me doing that, they take me to the Crisis Center and I end up in the hospital. Then I run away again. Nobody's going to make me live in a smelly old care home."

Jim, looking sharp in a suit and tie, speaks next. "I just want to thank all of you for praying for me. The Southwest Journal printed my article on the history of the first car dealer in Minneapolis. They paid me two cents a word. That's forty dollars. They want me to write some more."

Richard, an aged and weathered-faced Native American, piggybacks on Jim's words. I'm getting some help in writing my book. A student that works in the down town library helped me find some old papers that tell about Indian medicine men living in Minneapolis during the 1800s. They mention my family. She wants to help me get my story in writing. I'm getting so old and have days when I feel awful sick. Pray that God will help me get this done before I die."

Larry says, "Thanks, Richard, for sharing that with us."

"Ernest, what happened to your face? You don't look so good."

Ernest, an older lobotomy survivor in a worn-out gray trench coat, looks up through a swollen black eye. "I was waiting at the bus stop at Twenty-fourth Street and Hennepin Avenue when two fellows asked me for spare change. I told them I didn't have any money. Then they cornered me in the bus shelter and started pummeling me. The accused me of lying about not having money and kept working on me. Finally, a gentleman came by and called 911. They took me to the emergency room. I was there about four hours."

Whitey stands and shouts, "I would have taken my bike chain and beat them up. Did you press charges?"

"No, I wouldn't press charges. I told those guys, five or six times, that I forgave them for what they were doing, and if they killed me I still forgave them."

Whitey, still standing, shakes his head and asks, "Didn't you get mad?"

"What would I want to do that for? If I got angry, I would be doing the same thing they were doing. I hope they feel forgiveness and dignity in spite of what they did."

I speak next, "Ernest, after hearing your story, I feel I need to tell about an awful experience I had this week. Cathy called me, late at night, because her two kids had gone two days without milk or food. Rick had spent all their money on crack. He was waiting for me with a gun. He took my money and went to get more drugs. He said he didn't give a damn about the kids.

"He made me so mad. I heard voices in the back of my head saying, 'Kill him, kill him, kill him. Shoot him dead. The scum deserves to die.' Every part of me wanted to kill him. It scared me so badly that my whole body began shaking. I know those voices didn't come from God, but I think I really understand what some of you feel when you hear wild voices coming from your head.

"Pray for me. I want to be like Ernest in responding to the voice of God's love and not listening to my voices of anger and hate."

Larry says, "Does anyone else have anything to say? Are all hearts clear? Lars? Mark? Vickie? Al? Sallie? You all want to pass?"

Five heads nod.

Larry continues, "I want to thank you for your prayers and support over the last three months. You promised to pray about my addiction to cigarettes. You remember that I'd gone to the emergency room with a pain in my chest, and the doctors told me I had to stop smoking if I wanted to live much longer. I was so addicted to nicotine that it awakened me at night, demanding a smoke. I spent more on tobacco each week than I paid for food.

"Today it will be twelve weeks since I've smoked a cigarette, and I've started walking a mile each day. I'm so grateful to you and to God. Thank you! Thank God."

A comfortable silence of more than a minute follows.

Larry speaks again. "Before we have our prayer circle, I want to read some promises written by Saint Paul in the eighth chapter of Romans.

" 'For I am certain that nothing can separate us from his love: neither death nor life, neither angels nor other heavenly rulers or powers, neither the present nor the future, neither the world above nor the world below—there is nothing in all creation that will ever be able to separate us from the love of God...'

"This reminds us that God loves each one of us unconditionally. Disease, hurts, and problems do not come from God. They come from this crazy mixed-up selfish world we live in. There isn't anything we can do or say or think that's capable of driving away God's love. God is love. To know God is to know love. As we go to prayer, I ask you to think of yourselves as pulling the doors of your life open, wide, and letting God's love flow into your minds and bodies. Experience God's love."

FOUND SOULS

One Thursday morning at The Chef Café, as I finished my coffee, tuned out Allen's familiar tirade, and prayed for patience to get through the last ten minutes of our breakfast time together, I became keenly aware of his endless energy. Feelings within me reacted and I interrupted him with scolding words, "Allen, have you ever thought about putting your angry words into action? How about helping some of these people, like yourself, that have been rejected by family and society because of mental illness?"

Before I could finish the question, Allen stopped talking and began nodding his head in agreement.

The following week, I took him with me to a workshop in advocacy training conducted by the Mental Health Association of Minnesota. That day, Allen seemed to find a life mission. He quickly assumed the role of a mental health advocate. He failed to complete all the training sessions, but he started attending the monthly board meetings.

Before long, the board accepted his self-appointment and Allen began channeling his energies into helping persons with serious and persistent mental illness.

Allen's compulsive persistence did make things happen. Mental health providers and social agency directors feared Allen's angry screams and vitriolic attacks, because they respected his knowledge of mental health services and client rights. Social security workers knew that to deny or delay the claims of one of Allen's friends would subject them to daily harassment. He forced them to act in a correct and timely manner.

Allen's new role, together with my hours of listening, created a growing element of trust in Allen's mind. He felt accepted, and my status in his mind began to change from enemy to friend. He tested our relationship through repeated demands for help in the continual chain of scrapes and traumas his personality created. I passed his test.

Allen's psychiatrist, Dr. Freeburg, and his psychotherapist, Dr. Underwagger, skillfully and successfully led Allen to the realization that his problems stemmed from a broken brain, one that could not be fixed, and that consistent medication provided his only hope for a life outside the hospital. Repeated re-commitments when he neglected or overdosed on his medication reinforced the acceptance. I lost count of the number of times I escorted Allen to the Crisis Center to get him back on his medications or helped him get a handkerchief into his mouth so that his teeth would not be broken in med-reaction seizures.

One day I heard Allen announce to another schizophrenic, "Your problems come from a broken brain. It's not your fault. It's not your parent's fault." He still felt alone and abandoned. His anger still raged. He still ridiculed God. But the blame was gone.

It was a dramatic change. It was worth the hours I'd spent with him in restaurant booths.

One day I asked Allen if he would be willing to come to the Spiritual Life Fellowship and share his story. To my surprise, he agreed to attend. A greater surprise, he kept coming.

His pattern: talk, talk, talk during the coffee time preceding the group sessions, silent and quiet during the meetings, and loud talking after the closing prayer circle.

He did listen to the needs expressed by the persons in the weekly fellowships, and challenged them to accept his assistance.

Soon he became a self-appointed advocate and recruiter for the Spiritual Life Fellowships. Allen had concluded that the blaming of self and others for mental illness stemmed from a spiritual problem. He wanted his clients and friends to make the same discovery. He attended regularly and usually brought two or three others with him.

The week-by-week discussions in the Spiritual Life Group exposed participants to God's love. One by one, they began talking with fellow searchers from many religious, ethnic, and economic backgrounds who had discovered a new understanding of spirituality. Slowly, as they began sharing together, a love for God and other people replaced their old isolation, disconnectedness, and loneliness.

To my surprise, all the talk about love frightened and threatened Larry.

His keen mind had already concluded that a diseased brain caused mental illness. He challenged my limited thinking by quoting from books just off the press, like *The Broken Brain* by Nancy Andreason and *When Bad Things Happen to Good People* by Harold Kushner. But he couldn't recall a single personal experience of ever feeling loved.

His own past spiritual voices had been limited to the commands of the church and the pronouncements of pastors. With his bald head bowed and hands trembling, he shared with our group stories of condemnation, belittlement, humiliation, and rejection by pastors, teachers, colleagues, and "mama."

Stifled laughter spread through the room whenever someone, especially a woman, offered Larry a hug. He would shut his eyes, bow his head and tremble like a knight receiving the dub of a queen. After the event his timid face would radiate like that of an angel.

A value like love doesn't transmit well through lectures, but it can be learned through experience and absorbed through community. The fellowship of the group and the sharing of spiritual stories allowed seekers to renew old beliefs and experiment with new ones in a supportive and non-threatening environment.

Koinonia described the dynamic: the vertical dimension of the group member's love for and from God, and the horizontal dimension of the believer's love for and from others.

This deep spiritual community felt by group members as they gathered together emerged as a church experience. This "church" provided a context for spiritual growth by expecting, receiving, and sharing God's love.

Over time, the groups developed and consistently modeled what came to be called a Spiritual Discernment Program. Through this process, fellowship participants:

1) admitted a diagnosis of mental illness.
2) openly discussed God, prayer, and spiritual experiences.
3) rejected any attempt to equate the influence of God with naïve, ignorant, irrational, psychotic, or delusional thinking.
4) developed their own personal filters for separating spiritual influences from the disturbances of a disordered mind.
5) encouraged and reaffirmed their own personal, religious and moral values, and
6) discovered renewed faith.

The Spiritual Discernment Program helped group members to recognize the difference between the psychotic voice and the voice of God. The emerging consensus of the seven Spiritual Life Groups over a period of fifteen years might read something like this:

> The disordered voice feels angry, abusive, cold, distant, judging, and deadly.
> The Divine Voice feels calm, considerate, warm, intimate, accepting, and inspiring.
>
> The disordered voice feels demanding and reacts against all attempts to control it.
> The Divine Voice feels reciprocal—open to personal input and response.

The disordered voice feels manipulative and threatening.
The Divine Voice feels direct and gentle.

The disordered voice feels like ranting in a circular and repetitive form.
The Divine Voice feels definitive and directional.

The disordered voice feels interruptive, intrusive, and involuntary.
The Divine Voice feels patient, respectful, and inviting.

The disordered voice often feels grandiose, violent, and destructive.
The Divine Voice always feels humble, positive, constructive, and safe.

The disordered voice feels critical and rejecting.
The Divine Voice feels loving.

The groups agreed that love was the primary criterion of the Divine Voice.

MAD SAINTS

Intellectual conviction alone cannot bring spiritual healing, because every cell in the body has memory. The trauma endured by someone with mental illness has conditioned the entire organism. The research of A. Duncan Sinclair, who conducted many trauma studies, explains it this way: "When powerful memory is recalled, the gut remembers, the legs remember, the arms and fingers remember—our entire system remembers."

The sincere seeker with mental illness typically needs an orgasmic experience of God's love that is more powerful than the spiritual pain of their mental breakdown. This "falling in love" experience can then begin an ever-expanding relationship with God.

Psychiatrist Kenneth Pelletier has accumulated findings that prove what every one of us experiences every day: "that the mind and body are in inextricable interaction." Feelings like "love and compassion...fear and hostility, trigger powerful reactions in the body, which in turn both directly and indirectly affect blood chemistry, heart rate, activity in the stomach and gastrointestinal tract, activity of the immune system, and every other cell and organ in the body."

Studies with children diagnosed with a post-traumatic stress disorder prove that every organ, muscle, and cell of the body has memory and responds independently to pain.

When a child's old abuser enters the room, the victim's entire body cringes, even when the brain has blocked out any conscious memory of the event.

In his psychiatric dictionary, Robert Campbell supports the conclusion that the mind, "like other organs of the body, has its own local functions and those functions are intimately associated with adjacent and distant organs. It is like the cardiovascular system in that it reaches all parts of the body... and adjusts the total organism to needs and demands of the environment."

When John Wesley, the founder of World Methodism, experienced God he "felt his heart strangely warmed." His blood-pumping organ registered an increase in temperature as his emotions responded to the Divine presence.

Andrew Newberg and Eugene d'Aquili, leading figures in the emerging science that explores the links between spirituality and the brain, have used SPECT imaging to catch snapshots of the mind in the state of transcendence—mystical union with God.

These images indicate that an awareness of God stems from experience rather than thought. The moment of spiritual connection is as real to the nervous system as any physical perception. Newberg and d'Aquili suggest that our brains are literally "wired to experience the reality of God."

In short, God speaks to us through our brains, and the nervous system translates the communication into conscious awareness in the same way it processes all other information.

The diseased, damaged, retarded or broken brain challenges a person's ability to responsibly assess spiritual stimuli. But medication, therapy, training, and guidance can help the mentally ill person to receive, discern, and react appropriately to spiritual experiences.

The personal exploring of God's love occupies the final phase of spiritual reintegration. Re-conversion comes from an awareness of the unconditional love of God, receiving that love from God, and entering into a love connection with God. Fellowship participants entered into this experience by reducing spirituality to one simple truth: a love relationship with God.

What about each of these people's world-views, value systems, and moral guidance systems? Did all of these belief systems restore themselves—like the lost person seeing a familiar landmark and watching the entire landscape rotate into a recognized place? Yes, sometimes, but not often.

Instead, fellowship participants began to explore their new or renewed spiritual experiences.

Eventually I learned to offer participants two spiritual alternatives: they could either hold on to what they already knew or try to change. As psychologist Kenneth Pargament explains it, "the choice in coping is to conserve or to transform."

In conservation, some participants attempted to maintain what had been significant for them in the past. This usually was the preferred strategy.

In transformation, the participants developed, modified or revolutionized their beliefs and values.

When they asked me for advice, I consistently quoted the greatest commandment: "Love the Lord your God with all your heart and with all your soul and with all your mind." Often, I added, "Love your neighbor as yourself." Sometimes I helped them to clarify their own rituals, lifestyles, and moral philosophies.

With encouragement, most re-converts—over a period of weeks, months, and years—returned to affiliate with the churches, synagogues, denominations and religious groups where they had previously worshiped. The exceptions followed the influence of new spiritual friends.

Anger continually erupted as the greatest challenge to the renewal process. The pervasive mistreatment of the mentally ill had produced pathological hurt and resentment.

Deep bitterness clouded relationships with old friends, relatives, and religious groups.

Educator S. B. Simon cautions and reminds us, "These are more than just feelings. They represent coping devices aimed at conserving what is left of significance." These coping mechanisms did create spiritual problems. Anger reminded persons of their powerlessness. Hurt presented questions about personal worth. Resentment and hatred reflected the individual's great shame.

Love provided the only power capable of generating genuine forgiveness. Over time, the fellowship groups developed the love to forgive and love through forgiveness kept the groups alive.

Larry's encounter with God's love produced a conversion of his personality. The God voices began bombarding his mind with ego-building announcements. "You have value. You are worth more to me than the entire world. You are intelligent. You are capable. You have gifts and talents. You are a nice person. People like you. You are in this world for a reason. I have a plan for your life."

We watched Larry's shoulders pull back, his posture change, his eyes open, and his face smile as he shared these messages flowing from God.

The knowledge of God's unconditional love opened the mental trunk holding his old dreams. Eventually Larry felt that God recognized him as a theologian, and called him to follow through on his lifelong vision of becoming an ordained clergy.

On Thanksgiving Sunday, with all of the groups meeting together at Elliot Park for a potluck dinner and talent festival, Larry stood and announced, "God is calling me to do two things: start my own used bookstore and become ordained by the church."

At the time, I wondered how this diagnosed schizophrenic who received social security disability and lived in a subsidized hotel room, could achieve such ambitions. Part of me worried that both goals were grandiose schemes produced by a diseased and untrustworthy mind.

But what seemed unreachable began to unfold. The city condemned the old Andrews Hotel. The developers of the site agreed to relocate each tenant or, at their option, provide them each with a three thousand dollar transition grant. Larry exploited the opportunity.

I joined Larry the day he negotiated a rent contract with the owner of the storefronts at Twenty-second Street and Lyndale Avenue. We helped move the tables and shelves into Larry's Book Store. I installed a new shower in the basement living quarters.

That week he graduated from dependence to independence.

Larry knew books and their value. Within months, he and two part-time employees were supporting themselves by operating two successful bookstores on Lyndale Avenue.

Soon afterward, Larry became my associate and a group leader of the Fair Oaks and Elliot Park Fellowships. He registered for classes at North Central Bible College and enrolled in correspondence courses. After three years, he achieved his dream of ordination.

Allen entered the group environment of love like an immigrant to a new country. Frightened by relationships, he frantically searched for a new form of communication. Giving his time, energy, and attention to others out of a motivation of caring demanded a revolution of his thinking. He had learned to help others because "it's my job," "it's the right thing to do," and "I believe in justice."

Allen would spend an entire day finding a homeless person a place to live and food to eat. Or, he might help a handicapped client over a period of weeks to secure the evaluations and fill out the applications for social security disability. But when anyone attempted to return appreciation, kindness, or affirmation, it drove Allen into an emotional frenzy. Even sincere offers of friendship caused Allen deep frustration.

Treated as a misfit in a family devoid of love, he didn't know how to handle a simple person-to-person conversation. I doubt that he had honestly listened to one individual in his entire life.

But when he experienced true fellowship on a regular basis, his whole being began to respond. His initial attempts reminded me of a fourteen year old on a first date. But his determination produced a strange and rewarding result. He created a new family.

"Sallie is the mother, Denise is the daughter, and I am the father," Allen announced to our group one Sunday morning. The three had become acquainted through many weeks of playing gin together at Andrew Residence. Both women had major seizure disorders in addition to their mental illnesses.

Although about the same height and age as Allen, Sallie seemed much taller and more mature. As she explained, "I come from Oklahoma, where southern ladies know how to be decent and proper." Intolerant of rudeness, she could silence Allen when it would have been dangerous for anyone else to try.

Denise, physically in her twenties, enjoyed playing the role of a dependent twelve-year old. Allen doted on her like a grandfather.

The three became inseparable. Most days began with morning coffee at The Chef Café and ended with an evening dinner at Cicero's. If one of the trio had a doctor's appointment, they all went. If Allen had a meeting, Denise and Sallie waited patiently in the foyer or out in the car. They attended at least one fellowship meeting every Sunday as a family.

After Sallie left Andrew Residence for her own room at Pleasant Avenue Care Home, Denise moved into an assisted living apartment with Allen in Oak Grove Towers.

Allen introduced Sallie as his friend, not a girlfriend. He called Denise his "girlfriend," but consistently treated her as his little daughter.

Allen continued taking medication to control the voices in his head and kept his scheduled appointments with the doctors and therapists. He enthusiastically attended and promoted the fellowship groups every Sunday. Sometimes he would voice a quiet prayer during the closing circle. This very sick man had found peace with God and himself.

The following June, he requested Baptism at the annual ecumenical service held at Lake Nokomis. Chaplain John Owen asked, "Do you believe in God, the Father Almighty, the maker of heaven and earth? And in Jesus Christ, His only begotten Son, our Lord?" Allen responded: "All this I firmly believe."

Soon afterwards Allen's anger stopped.

For me, after being on the receiving end of more than four years of Allen's abuse, it felt like the calm following a Minnesota tornado.

I don't know how it happened. I asked Sallie and Denise. They could only shake their heads. Over a period of about three weeks the roaring simply disappeared. Calm conversation replaced the anticipated screams. The threatening phone calls ceased. The rage had escaped.

Allen greeted others in the fellowship with a hug and the words, "I love you."

When asked about his faith, Allen would announce, "I am a Jew who believes in Jesus Christ" and "I am a child of God and a follower of Jesus."

In November, after his June Baptism, Allen asked for a conference with the church superintendent, treasurer, and District Board. He presented a copy of his personal will and testament. He wanted his share of the family estate placed in a trust designated to support Minneapolis programs for people with mental illness.

Allen's father died in 1980. Unaware that the parents had legally disinherited their only son, Allen assumed he would divide the sixteen million dollar legacy with his sister when their mother died.

Things took a dramatic change during the next year, when doctors diagnosed Allen with colon cancer. He came home from the hospital to a mature Denise. In less than three weeks she changed from a submissive child to a responsible, care-giving adult, making decisions for the household, expertly changing Allen's colostomy bags, and providing daily nursing care. Allen complied without protest.

Fascinated with trains, he asked Denise to join him in traveling by Amtrak to Seattle, down the West Coast, and back to Chicago to visit family. Denise assumed full responsibility in the planning and management of the trip and those final days.

Early, on the morning of Independence Day, Denise heard tornado sirens and attempted to rouse Allen. He refused to respond. She called her dad. He called 911. The paramedics arrived and pronounced Allen dead. He was forty-three years old.

At Allen's memorial service, his mother handed me a check made out to the Spiritual Life Group for two thousand dollars. The family flew his body back to Palm Springs for burial.

At the service, Denise read her tribute:

"I was crushed, shocked, and sad. I stopped going to church. Part of me believed in God. The rest of me was in darkness. I couldn't understand what God was doing in my life. I was so mixed up. I didn't care if I lived or not. I tried suicide many times but it never seemed to work. When I went into Andrew Board and Care Home I met Allen. Allen and I were very close. It was through him that I began attending the Fair Oaks Fellowship. When Allen had cancer surgery, my life really changed. By the time he died eight months later, I was really close to the Lord. His love made me feel like a worthwhile person. Because God lives and Allen is living with him, I can face tomorrow."

"Pastor, this is Melanie. I'm not at home. I won't be at my house when you come to see me. I'm at Ruth's apartment."

"At Ruth's place?" I asked. "How in the world did that happen?"

"Well, remember how in our group last Sunday, I told about Sheldon being so mean to me? Well after I got home, I get this call from Ruth. She tells me that she loves me. She actually said those words. And she wanted me to know that if I felt I needed to get away from my husband, I could come and live with her.

"At first, I told her I didn't think it would work out. You know how critical she's been...always bawling me out and blaming me for everything.

"But something happened. She's changed. She cooks my meals. Waits on me hand and foot. She treats me like I'm a princess of some kind. And she listens to me.

"And you won't believe this...she heard that a single parent down the hall couldn't go to work because she wasn't able to hire a baby sitter. She offered to take care of this little girl every day this week."

A few hours later I knocked on the door of apartment 33. A softened Ruth opened the door and invited me in. Nickie, a little three year old clutched the skirt and called her "Gammy Ruth." The impossible had happened.

In December, Ruth invited me to a holiday party she hosted for the residents of Chicago Avenue Apartments. In less that two months, she had become everyone's friend. Ruth introduced me to each of the residents in the community room announcing, "I'm a different person because of the loved of the people in our fellowship."

In the months that followed, Ruth created a new Spiritual Life Group by reaching out to the persons with mental illness in her three building housing complex. It soon outgrew the apartment, moved to the nearby community center, and became the Elliot Park Spiritual Fellowship.

A new energy flowed through Ruth. After becoming active in the Park Avenue Senior Center, she began to paint. Impressed, the owner of Danny's Bar invited her to display her work in a public showing.

Three weeks before Ruth died of cancer, I found her sister standing with a pastor in the hospital corridor outside the hospice room. As I walked by them and approached Ruth's bed, she shouted, "They came here asking me to pray the sinner's prayer and get ready for heaven. They want me to rejoin the Zion Lutheran Church. I haven't seen them in twenty years and now they come here to tell me I'm going to hell. I told them to go back home and leave me alone."

She reached, found my hand, grasped it, and smiled. She said, "I love God and God loves me. That's all of the religion I want and need."

PAPA'S BROKEN TOY

Sallie's Story

MAMA

A Mosquito Made Mama Mad

"Mama, why are you mad at me?" I asked.

"You silly child, I'm not mad at you. Why do you think that way?"

I looked at the floor and whispered, "I don't know."

But I remembered the song on my bright yellow Christmas record. It played to me the words, "As for me, my little brain isn't very bright. Bring to me, dear Santa Claus, what you think is right."

Let me tell you how the little brain knew it wasn't bright. It heard mama and papa talking. My spells put me out but my ears kept working. I heard mama's voice speaking like a radio under water. She said, "Why do you keep hurting me?" and "Sallie, stop doing do this to us." How could I do anything to her when I was lying flat on the floor, jerking like my dying rabbit?

I knew mama hated me, because she didn't want people seeing her with the little monster. I went to a special school some days. Mama stayed home alone. She never left the house. I made her feel ashamed. If a neighbor called asking us to visit, mama said a polite "no" and explained by telling my story.

Mama says I came into the world a beautiful little baby, her only child. I smiled like the sun. I was smart as a whip. She called me her precious angel. I made her happy as a lark.

Then, one little mosquito stung me.

Did you know that it is only the female mosquito that sticks a person and sucks the blood?

That mosquito spit a virus into my blood. It gave me eastern equine encephalomyelitis. Let me spell it: E-N-C-E-P-H-A-L-O-M-Y-E-L-I-T-I-S. See, it's written here in my little book. Mama wished I had died like most babies who get sickness from a mosquito. The children who live end up with mental problems, epilepsy, and palsies, like me.

My head and mind did not work like other girls'. Seizures struck me like lightning every day. Some little ones were not so bad, but a few left me passed out. You know what a seizure is? Mama told me, "It makes all your muscles jerk and keep on jerking."

I could hear the seizures coming. The buzzing sound started in my head and thundered like a train getting closer. My brain doctor called those warnings auras. He showed me how to keep a tiny diary. I wrote a note each time I had an aura, a seizure and a big grand mal. They made my memory disappear, just like erasing a blackboard. When that happened I had to open the little brain book to find out where I should be and what I was supposed to be doing.

Mama faced the mornings like making ready for a funeral. She poked holes in each day by hissing a sigh and saying, "This, too, will pass." It kept her from closing the drapes on her life.

My mama stayed mad until she died. She hated the mosquito, all the people with healthy babies, and me. She felt life had run her over. Like my injured puppy, she waited to be put out of her misery.

Mama died young because of my problem and her funeral buried me in fears. Each year, near the time mama died, I got so sick I had to stay in a hospital.

The mosquito bit me but it gave mama and papa a "hate God" virus. They believed in God before my fever. As a pretty little baby, they took me to church for baptism. The blood-sucking bug changed everything. "I can never forgive God for what happened to my little girl," Mama cried. "A loving God would not let mosquitoes bite little girls and make them crazy."

"Is Mama right in saying that my problem is God's fault?" I asked Papa.

He shook his head, "I don't really know. I just don't believe in God anymore."

"How could one little mosquito drive me mad," I wondered, "and make my mama mad at me, at all the people in our world, at herself, and even at God?"

My thoughts have changed. I'm not mad at God anymore. I know I'm dying, but I'm not afraid. I love God. I'm waiting to meet God in Heaven.

It all began when I met Allen.

ALLEN

Mad Allen Met Mad Me

Mama died and I didn't know what to do or where to go. I fell out of my little nest. It scared my mind. Seizures wiped me out all day long. I screamed and cried. I had to stay in the hospital for a whole year.

Mama had hid her injured little bird in our house for thirty-eight years. Each day unwound the same. Papa dragged himself home from work late at night. I slipped on his slippers. Mama served him a warmed-over supper. We watched the news and went to bed. Papa left in the morning, early. When I had problems, mama cried. I screamed because mama bawled. We kept a cloud of silence around papa. It saved us from his storms.

Mama got terrible sick. I stayed in the hospital swimming in drugs while she passed away.

Papa exploded. "You can't come back home. I can't take care of you with mama gone."

"You have a problem." Dr. Underwagger told Papa.

"I don't pay you shrinks a hundred dollars an hour to tell me it's my fault and not Sallie's," Papa said.

"The hospital is kicking you out, like a stray," the doctor joked. He sent me to Andrew Care Home, a place for mad strays.

Andrew scared me speechless. Too many crazy people, all sick like me. Two hundred handicapped persons in one home, packed three to a room. The crowds made me squeal and run like a wounded bunny. They herded the residents into a big dining room to eat. I hid and starved in my burrow.

The good thing for me was I met angry Allen. He was schizophrenic. The staff called him Mad Al, because he was always yelling about something. Everybody in Minnesota knew Allen, including the governor and the mayor. He belonged to the Alliance and worked as an advocate for the mentally ill. Allen spent each day going to meetings and screaming at important people on the phone. He hissed and flapped like a big mean gander.

Allen thought important people listened to him because of his millionaire parents. They owned a big business in Minneapolis. You know him and his folks. His grandparents' mansion still stands on Park Avenue.

He lived on SSI just like me, but his papa and mama gave him spending money of one thousand dollars per month and a credit card. He owned a new car, a cream-colored Chrysler LeBaron Convertible with red leather seats. His meds made him drive like a drunken blind man. It scared the police and me but he didn't have any bad accidents.

Allen dressed in a dark expensive suit and tie, which didn't fit very well over his fat middle. His black hair and clothes were always messy. He looked like a penguin that had been hit by a truck, but I liked him. If he got mad at me, I just shut my mouth. Before the day ended, he would forgive and forget.

Allen came to Andrew with a pastor. He told us "I am a Jew and a Christian"—a Jew who believed in Jesus Christ. He helped the pastor start a Spiritual Life Group.

Allen lived to take care of people. He thought I needed him. He said he could help me get moved to a home where I could stay in my own room. He became my friend.

Allen had a friend named Denise. He called her his little girl. She had seizures just like me. He moved her out of Andrew to live with him in his apartment. They slept together in the same bed, but they didn't ever do anything. Allen couldn't because of the Haldol.

For eight years the three of us hung together every day. "Allen is the Papa, Sallie is the Mama, and Denise is the little girl," people said. I had a new family.

Allen took us out to eat at Cicero's each evening and we went to the fellowship every Sunday.

Allen got sick with colon cancer and Denise changed. She grew into a strong nurse taking care of her dying friend. She didn't need a papa and mama anymore.

Allen died soon after his forty-fifth birthday. Denise was in bed with him. She heard the tornado sirens and tried to wake Allen. He was dead.

Allen's death filled me with black cold thoughts. But like mama I kept saying, "This, too, will pass."

Denise showed me how faith in God keeps death from being scary.

MEN

Men Made Me Mad

My friend Allen changed my feelings about men.

Papa refused to let me come back home. He threw me away. "I hate, hate, hate men," I said. Still, I cried and cried because I loved papa so much and wanted to be with him.

After that, men frightened me. I saw God as a big and powerful man who was mean to me and made me sick.

"Don't trust men. They just want sex. Leave them alone" Mama had warned me.

It mixed up my mind. I wanted to have a boyfriend, do sex, get married and be a mother. But men made me mad and afraid. That's the way my little mind thought.

Allen became my first man friend. I trusted him, even though he was big, powerful, and sometimes mean. He took care of me until the day he died. "Maybe God is someone like Allen," I thought.

I met my first boyfriend in my fortieth year. I didn't care for Ted, but he really wanted me. I liked the feeling of being needed by a man. He kept me safe from all the sick men at Andrew. Once I was with Ted, other guys quit bothering me.

We dated. Mostly, we went out with my friends, like Allen and Denise. We started having sex. After a while, I wanted it worse than he did, I think. The medications kept him limp and that made him very angry.

The doctor heard about our sex and urged me to get my tubes tied. Ted and I liked it better after the surgery. It stopped our worrying.

We had many fights. His messing around with other girls made me angry. We didn't have many good days because either he was mad at me or I was mad at him. The counselor called it a poor relationship. It felt right when I moved out of Andrew and into my own room at the Pleasant Avenue Home.

Kim lived upstairs there. He came into my room one night. I guess I knew why he was there, but I didn't care. He didn't ask me for a date. He walked over to me, sitting in the rocking chair that used to be my mama's, put his arm around me, and started rubbing my back.

"You afraid?" he asked.

"No" I said.

"Is this OK with you?" he whispered.

"Yes," I whispered back.

We hugged and kissed a long time. It made me hungry to have sex with him. It didn't feel wrong. I was starving for sex with a man that could really do it.

"Do you want me to take off my blouse?" I asked.

"Yes," he said.

"Do you want me to take it all off?"

"Yes, Sallie, take it all off." He was breathing real fast.

I liked it when he stroked me. I got it. "Wow! How nice!" I thought. He got it before we went all the way. We started all over. It worked better for both of us the second time.

I never saw Kim again. He told me he shouldn't do it because I was a "vulnerable adult" and he could get arrested.

A few months later they found him out at Wirth Park. He had committed suicide. I think of him and wonder if I made him kill himself.

I met Rodney at the Fellowship. He came from the state hospital in Yankton, South Dakota. The doctors wanted the University to fix his head. It swelled up with too much water. A big tube drained stuff from his brain. The shaved hair made him look like a Martian.

He read the Bible and prayed a lot. He talked about feeling close to God. He liked the Fellowship meetings but missed the church back home.

He loved me and I loved him. But his medication kept us from being lovers.

He died eight months after we met. I went to the hospital every day to see him. He had a strong faith. I wanted to believe in God, like Rodney.

I was mad at him for dying and leaving me alone. But I knew that a man loved me and I loved a man.

I didn't feel as mad at Papa then, and my fear of God began to go away.

I remembered Mama saying, "This, too, will pass," and I hoped for the day when God would love me.

SAINTS

Mad Saints and Lost Me

Allen drove Denise and me to the Spiritual Fellowship on Sundays. It met in the lower level banquet room of the Fair Oaks Motel and Restaurant over by the Art Institute. Allen showed me a list of many board and care centers in that neighborhood. He took flyers and invitations to each person in every home. A lot of people came. Most of them had mental problems just like me. Denise and I volunteered to make the coffee and help fix the lunch.

The Fellowship changed my ideas about church. We sat together in a big circle drinking coffee. We started by singing along with the spiritual songs on tape. We could request our favorites. I liked "The Rose" by Bette Midler and "You Need a Friend" by Carole King. Denise asked for gospel choruses.

The leader let each person in the circle answer the question, "How are things going in your personal spiritual life?" The sharing of feelings lasted for two hours.

"I pass," I said, joining the others that didn't choose to talk. I didn't say anything but I listened a lot.

People came because they wanted to learn more about God. They wanted to hear from people who had known God for months and years. I had questions about God ringing in my mind, but was too scared to ask them. Still, I found answers by hearing others tell their stories.

Most of the people had followed some religion at an earlier time in their lives, but lost faith when they started having mental problems. An older lady believed the Ba` hai religion. "I am a Gypsy," one woman announced. She worshiped Satan.

The Fellowship closed with prayer together. The people in the group joined hands in a circle while they prayed for everything from help for a dying loved one to the healing of a sick pet.

I hid in my corner like a little mouse facing a room full of cats. At one of those first meetings, I started screaming, ran out the door, and had a grand mal right there in the hall. What gave me the courage to keep coming? I don't know. I joined in the circle after three years of watching and sitting like a statue, unable to speak.

I learned to accept people. I felt loved by these friends. The group helped me reach the place where I could work with others in a part time job.

The pastor met with me over coffee each week. All I needed to do was say, "I need time," and he set an hour for us to meet together. I felt I could share all my feelings with him. I treasured those special times. I knew he believed in me. He loved and accepted me.

The first day I shared followed ten years of listening.

"Today I feel able to trust God," I said. "This week, during the funeral of my papa, God's love came into my life. I know God loves me and I love God. I understand what you have been talking about all these years. I am a believer."

PAPA

Mad Papa, Lost Me

Papa got mad at God and me when I changed from a pretty little baby to a screaming brat with lots of seizures. I remember him coming to my room and talking to me. He tried to be nice, but he acted like a tiger waiting to escape. That's how I knew he hated me. He got angry every time we talked.

Mama told me that Papa worked long hours every day because coming home made him nervous. I knew what she meant: he didn't want to face me.

Papa treated me like a broken toy. He couldn't play with me unless I got fixed.

"Someday Sallie will be well," he said as he took me to see another doctor.

Papa found some teachers at the university who wanted to try a new kind of operation. The doctor said he could cut off some of the bad brain. If they killed the bad part, then the good part could start thinking right. They cut a big hole in my skull. It is still there. If I touch the top of my head, I don't feel any bone, just skin and hair over a soft place. Papa believed this surgery would cure me.

It didn't help. The seizures got worse, and I lost a lot more of the remembering part of the brain. That's when Papa gave up. He junked me like a car beyond repair.

It hurt me awful when Mama died and Papa sent me away from home.

"I can make dinner and bring your slippers, just like Mama," I said.

"No, I don't want you at home," he said. "I can't take care of you."

I didn't see him for a long time.

Papa finally came to see me. He brought Nellie with him. Nellie lived next door to us. Papa and Nellie talked to each other over the side-yard fence for many years. Then Nellie's husband passed away. Nellie was alone and Papa was alone. Papa told me, "Like lovebirds, we've decided to quit sitting on the fence, get married, and move into a cage together."

I liked Nellie. She cared for me like a true mama. She coaxed Papa to come and spend time with me. Nellie talked to me. Papa sat and listened. She treated me like a visible person.

Nellie belonged to the Mt. Olivet Lutheran Church. They held a Mental Health Sunday each year and formed support groups for the parents of kids with broken brains. As a nurse, Nellie understood the problems of mental patients. She helped Papa accept and love me like a special daughter.

Papa got terrible sick with cancer and started going to church with Nellie. He came to visit and invited me out to Nellie's house. He didn't get angry anymore. Sadness took the place of his madness.

Papa changed before he died. He became a believer and joined the church.

At the funeral, the pastor told the family that Papa died ready to go to heaven and meet with God. I think God forgave Papa for hating me when Papa forgave me for being a sick daughter.

Last February my brain quit working. I wandered in the cold and snow for three days and nights. They found me walking down Vernon Street where Nellie lives. I tried to find her place.

"Sallie is disoriented times three," the paramedics said. That meant I had forgotten my name, I couldn't tell the time, and I didn't know where I lived.

The emergency doctor found the tumor in my head.

I told Nellie, "This, too, will pass." But it didn't.

GOD

Lost Me Found God

I'm glad you came. It helps for me to talk. I need to finish my story. I won't be able to move my lips much longer.

How can you stand to see me? My head and face have swollen so big. In my mirror I see a stranger who looks like the fat woman in a circus. I push this medicine button to kill the pain but it doesn't keep me from growing ugly.

Does it seem weird to you? I lived with mental problems all my life, and now I'm dying with a tumor on the brain. I always figured I would get cancer. Mama got it and died so young. Then Papa. Do you think my brain surgery and strong meds started it all? I guess it doesn't matter now. Does it?

Today I want to talk about God.

Remember the Sunday I came to fellowship, and told the group, "I felt the presence of God at Papa's funeral and now God seems very close to me"? Since that time, I've felt God's love with me every day.

I know you loved me, Pastor. The Fellowship people loved me. You told me over and over, "God loves you, just like you are." But my thoughts began to change when Nellie and Papa started loving me.

At Papa's funeral, I knew that God really loved me. I stopped seeing myself as a sick stray cat. A lot of the stress went away. The doctor told me that getting upset made my seizures worse, but he didn't tell me how to keep from being scared. God helped me. The grand mals quit coming. I still heard the auras, but the seizures stopped.

I started going to the Vocational Service Program. Before long, I worked every day. Finally, they made me a trainer. I supervised the team and checked the work.

I wanted to leave the Aldrich Care Home. I didn't need a nest any longer. I could fly on my own.

Ann, my social worker, introduced me to Audrey and the foster care program. Audrey invited me to live with her.

I moved out of the city and into Audrey's Richfield home. I didn't feel like a mental anymore. I still took all of the medicines. SSD and MSI paid my bills. I had a social worker. But I saw myself as a normal person, living and working like everyone else. It made me so happy. I felt like a robin singing in the springtime.

Remember when you picked me up at Audrey's, took me to Perkins, and we celebrated?

That same week, on Sunday, I visited Hope Church. I simply walked in and sat in the back seat by myself. Imagine me, being able to sit in that pew with hundreds of other people. After the worship, Irene came and sat down beside me. She wanted to get acquainted. Each Sunday after that, she came and sat with me. Before long we moved up a few rows and joined with the regular churchgoers. The pastor shook my hand after each service. He treated me like a member of the congregation.

I saw a little card in the church folder asking for volunteers. It told about the "Church Home" program. Hope Church joined with fifty-two other groups; each congregation agreed to house and feed homeless families for one week. They turned the church into a dormitory for families and singles with no place to eat and sleep. They needed someone to scrub and clean after the people moved on to the next church. That's what I did at VSP, so I put my name down.

I knew some of the homeless people that came to stay in the church. I met them while I lived at Andrew. Think of that. God used me to help people with problems just like me. That night I thanked God for helping me change my life.

Pastor Talley heard about my training and chose me to clean his study and office. He needed a trustworthy, dependable person. He gave me my own key.

I decided to take the membership class and join the church.

Pastor Talley from Hope plans to lead the funeral. I asked him to have you speak at the service. Is that OK with you?

This could be the last time we talk. I may not live another week. If we don't meet again, I will see you in the other world.

I know God loves me. I know I love God. I'll soon be in heaven. Allen will be there. I'll see Mama and Papa. Remember how I used to fall apart when anyone died? Now I am not afraid. I just say to myself, "This, too, will pass."

DANNY BOY AND DADDY O

Danny's Story

DANNY BOY DREAMS

"Pastor, come in. Come in. Please come in. I'm so excited. I really am excited to see you. I think I told you. I did. Didn't I? Maybe I didn't. I thought I told you on the phone. I found the folder. I found this flyer under the door. I placed it here on the table. It tells about the fellowship. See, Cedar Riverside Fellowship.

"But I can't go out. I won't go out. People watch me. They look at me. They try to hurt me. They all talk about me. They laugh at me. My fundamental problem, I am paranoid. It started when I was at Harvard. Yes, I did go to Harvard. Did you know I went to Harvard? How would you know I went to Harvard? I had to leave there and come home. They laughed at me. I couldn't let them laugh at me.

"So, I thought—no, God told me. God said, call this number. Talk to this pastor and ask him to come meet with me. Just me. Nobody else. Just me. God wants to make a fellowship of just two—you and me.

"I'm all alone. I'm completely alone. I don't have anyone. I'm happy all alone, but I don't have anybody. I need a friend. I need one friend. I need a friend that prays like me. You know, a God friend, a real friend.

"Have a seat. Take a chair. I'm so glad you came. Here, you sit on the couch and I'll sit in my own chair. We can talk like friends."

`"Well, Danny, it's a pleasure to meet in person. You have a cozy little place here. It's not like the apartments in the towers; you have a nice view of the courtyard."

"I moved into this apartment last June. I like residing on the plaza. No one lives above me to disturb me like phantoms in the night. And no one lives below me to complain about my roaming insomnia. People live on either side but they don't interfere with me and I ignore them. I feel protected here."

"It does feel quiet and secure here. That's important when you're living all alone. Danny, you say that you need a friend. Don't you have any friends? How about your family? Do they live here in the cities?"

Pastor, did I tell you my last name is McFadden? Did I mention that? We're McFaddens. That's Irish, you know. Do you know that? There are more than fifty McFaddens named in the phone book, but not one from my family. I did have a mother. They committed her to Willmar State Hospital, but she died two years ago."

"What about your father, Danny?"

"My father lives in Michigan. I don't have recent information. I vacationed with him when I went to Stony Brook and then Harvard. I left the university after I became ill. Did I tell you that I have paranoid schizophrenia and an obsessive-compulsive disorder? Do you remember? Did I reveal that on the phone? Did I tell you that at the door? He came to my mother's funeral. I have no contact with my father. I probably told you that already.

"You're a pastor, right? You're a man of prayer. I need someone to pray with me. You keep things confidential, right?"

"Yes, Danny, pastors keep things confidential, but I must tell you that I'm required to reveal anything illegal or dangerous. If I think you might hurt yourself or someone else, I must make a report. Otherwise, I promise to hold everything in confidence. What do you want me to do? How can I help you?"

"Pastor, I want to make a contract. Like when the therapist asks me to make a verbal contract. I want to contract with you to come and see me once a week for fellowship. You'll be my companion. I'll be your companion. We'll be friends. We'll share and then pray. Could you do that? I read about your Sunday fellowships. But I can't come. I can't leave this room. I go see my psychiatrist once a month. A cab comes to get me."

"I could make one visit a week to talk about spiritual things and pray with you. But how do you live? What about food? What about clothes and laundry? How do you survive, alone in this apartment?"

"It's easy, Pastor. You said you were Pastor Orin? No, I won't call you Pastor. I'll call you Daddy. You asked about my father, so you can be my daddy. I'm going to call you Daddy O. Daddy O, Daddy O, Daddy O, I like that.

"Daddy O, I have my groceries and medicines delivered to my door. My social worker visits once a month and she has Alma come to clean each week. She says I'm abandoned. Abandoned? Not abandoned. Not abandoned. I'm independent and secluded. Maybe neglected? But not abandoned.

"I have my own kingdom here. Let me show you.

"I present you seven years of collector excursions. Cast your eyes on my collections. The walnut cases covering the south wall contain all the classics. Have you studied the classics? I specified the deluxe binding with gold imprint. Behold the impressive gold letters. I possess every volume produced by the Classics of the Month Club. I examined the complete catalog. I own the complete collection. I touch them. I care for them. I keep them clean. I read them.

"We can study them together, Daddy O. I'll listen as you expound. We'll engage in a reading fellowship. How literate are you? Do you consider yourself well read? Have you explored the classics?"

"A few, Danny, but certainly not all. I recognize some of the names from the authors game we used to play when I was a kid. It would be nice to read together. We could meet once a week and you could teach me about these great writers."

"Good. Now, Daddy O, feast your intellect on these volumes in the special green case. Observe. Recognize these names: Yeats, Russell, Joyce, Shaw, the famous writers from Ireland. I think of these authors as my Irish ancestors. I'm of Irish heritage. Irish. Grandpa and Grandma, Father and Mother, they're all descended from Irish stock. Mother desired to vacation with me in Ireland. She planned to escort me to Ireland. Then she became terminally ill. The fantasy of her last days included a journey to Ireland.

"I have the photo album we created together. We collected photos of our favorite Irish places. Come over here by the desk and glance at them. Let me open the book of our dreams. We slipped our favorite scenes into these pages.

"Here, let me show you. Imagine viewing the Ring of Kerry right across the page from the Limerick city on the River Shannon. Now, this is

Connemara and the Twelve Bens. And on the next page is the lake-isle of Innisfree, that's in Lough Gill, near Sligo Town. And, over here, the Wicklow Hills and Glenveagh Park on the banks of Lough Veagh.

"We anticipated flying to Ireland and touring all the scenic areas. Then mother died. I told you she passed on. Didn't I inform you of her death? I must have. Yes, you asked about my mother and I told you. She's gone, but I talk to her, each day, in prayer."

"I'm sorry about your mother. It sounds like you had a close relationship with her. Do you miss her a lot? Did she like the Irish writers? Did you share these books together?"

"Mother never enrolled in college. Did I tell you that I went to Harvard? I didn't tell you that, did I? I never completed the course work. And I couldn't graduate. I became ill and had to leave. That depressed mother. She wanted me to be educated.

"Reading frustrated Mother, but she loved my music. Good music. Classical music. She worshiped my collection of classical music.

"Check this out, Daddy O... the east wall of cabinets. Behind these doors rest all of Mother's favorite recordings. Focus on the titles of these 33 l/3 rpm stereo albums. We reveled in them.

"All the great names appear: Schuman, Brahms, Tchaikovsky, Haydn, Bach, Bizet, Mozart, Schubert, Handel, Chopin, Vivaldi, Liszt, Beethoven and, of course, we have our patron Irish composer, John McCormack.

"Mother curled up on the sofa and I reclined with my feet up on the ottoman. We relaxed and listened to an entire album without saying a word. Quiet, silent, we didn't twitch or fidget until it was done.

"We could do that, Daddy O. I don't require therapy. I don't desire a counselor. I simply wish you to be my friend. We could be a true fellowship of two. Would you consent to doing that? I prayed and God told me to dial the phone and invite you. I did explain, didn't I? God commissioned me to form a fellowship of two, here, in my little place with you. But I already told you that.

"Daddy O, let me explain my meditation moments. I place an album on the stereo, select one volume of a bound classic, position it on my little prayer bench, kneel, listen, and read. When the album ends, I put the book away, select a scripture reading, contemplate, and pray.

"I communicate with God on this prayer table each day. See this ornate bench? It's my little altar. The Wood Carving Shop on West Lake Street created this prayer table at my request. They crafted it according to the specifications I prepared. They arranged each set of legs in the shape of a cross. See the little crosses? They made it the proper height. I'm able to kneel on this soft rug, rest my elbows on its smooth polished top, relax, meditate, and pray. Mother meets me here. I ruminate for hours, right here, on my knees each day. God's revelations appear. I relate to him and he communicates with me.

"God directed me to contact you. While kneeling at my prayer table, God revealed himself and ordained me to begin a new fellowship with you. I did tell you, didn't I? Yes, I did. I'm sure I already mentioned that to you. Will you do it, pastor? Will you be my Daddy O and start a fellowship with me?"

"Yes, Danny, it would be nice to come for an hour each week. I could relax with you, read, listen, talk, and pray, with no other agendas. But don't you have any friends? Don't you know anyone?"

"My only friend has been smiling upon us every moment. Contesse, beautiful Contesse, my lover Contesse. Observe Contesse's beautiful eyes; they follow your movements across the room. I sense Contesse's love. Contesse is my constant companion. Whenever I glance up, from anywhere in the room, I see Contesse. I decorated the other three walls with the Ireland greens of Keating and Sullivan, but I reserved the center for Contesse, my love.

"Have you met her? Do you know her? Have you had the pleasure of her company? Have you met Contesse d'Haussonville? Here, turn and look at her. Look into her eyes.

"Jean Auguste Dominique Ingres, the great French artist, created her in oil on canvas in 1845. She came from New York City and the Frick Collection of full-sized prints. She vowed to never leave me.

"Each morning I caress her hand, the hand with the ring. See, the hand with the ring. I touch her hand and look into her eyes and say, 'My Contesse, I love you. I love you. I love you. I love you.' I love her. I love her. I love her. Sweet, innocent, lovely Contesse loves me. She loves me."

"Danny, it's been a pleasure to meet you. I'm impressed and overwhelmed by your knowledge of the arts. I would like to spend an hour each week listening, learning, and praying. We can plan to meet each Friday at three. Let's try it and see how it goes."

DANNY BOY DARES

"Daddy O, come in. Come in. I've been anticipating your presence. You were absent last week and it made me depressed. Do come in. I have Haydn on the machine. We finished the Handel album when you visited the last time. So far we've experienced Bach, Bizet, Brahms, and Chopin together. The next entrée is Haydn. Did I tell you that Haydn's music is playing? Yes, I told you that when you first opened the door. I must have given you that information.

"I brewed some tea. Please be seated on the couch. I'll be seated in the chair this time. I've been praying the last two hours and I need a change of position. Usually I prefer kneeling, but today I have a proposition for you. I have something extremely important to share with you today. I planned to wait until after our music and meditation, but it seems extremely important, extremely important. I have something very important to tell you. The tea can wait. God has given me an inspiration. More than an inspiration, a revelation, an extremely important revelation from God.

"It gives me great excitement. It interrupted my meditation. It races through my mind at night when I should be sleeping. Each evening, after my day of reading, listening, and meditation I make my supper and do the dishes. Then I sit and dream. My lips whisper, 'Ireland, O Ireland.' I think of the Emerald Isle. I walk over to each of the landscapes on the wall. I caress each different shade of green with my fingers. I dream of experiencing these scenes with my own eyes.

"Now God has given me an imperative. God expects me to walk by faith. I have a divine vision. It frightens me to think about it, but I'm compelled. I need your assistance. I need your strength. I need your time. You must help me. You will help me, won't you?

"Oh, I haven't told you yet. Here I'm asking for a commitment and you don't even have the information.

"God has given me a vision, a miracle vision. I'm perspiring, look at me... anxious, wringing my hands, and perspiring. See how nervous I am? The perspiration flows from every pore.

"God has ordained me to go to the land of luscious green. I've acquired some money. My social worker advises me to do a spend-down to meet the requirements of the disability payments. A frugal three months and I'll have the money to do it. Two weeks of freedom strolling with mother across Ireland. It's my last chance, my only hope. I must go."

"Danny, I'd like you to think about what you're proposing. You can't even go to a grocery store because there are too many people for you. Have you any idea of the crowds of people in the airport? You left the hospital because you couldn't be in the same room with another person; now you want to spend a day jammed in a plane with three hundred passengers. You never make it to your doctor's appointment on time; how can you keep up with a tour schedule? You'd be left behind at the first rest stop.

"Danny, you know I'm your friend. We have been meeting together for three months. I want to support you and we've been praying that you'll feel better. But this is too much. Maybe we could take a walk or go to a movie a few times, first, and then we could talk about Ireland."

"Daddy O, I'm determined to go. I have the underlined travel folder in my hand. It says right here. I have the plan right here. See the schedule right here? Here it is. One direct flight over, one bus trip, one cab to my village inn, one return cab to the bus, the bus to the airport, one flight home. I have the ability. I can maintain that long.

"And, look here, look here, Daddy O. See this book? Look at the cover. It proclaims, 'Hill walking, the popular sport of Ireland.' It shows the hiking trails from the inn. I will hike one trail each day, one trail each day, one trail each day. Mother will be with me. Mother will help me. Just like we planned three years ago. Will you help me? I implore you. You keep telling me that you're my friend and that God loves me. God wants me to go on this journey. God wants you to help me prepare.

"Will you help me plan, Daddy O? Join me in dreaming and planning together, please. I want to do this. I want your help. I have a list of my necessities. I solicit your commitment. If you truly love me, if you truly care, if you are sincerely my friend, then please do this one thing for me."

"Danny, you need to do these things yourself. But I'll tell you what. If you can get everything you need—plane tickets, passport, and all that—I'll help you get ready for your dream trip.

"Danny, I'm afraid that you'll get on an airplane or a bus and fall apart. If you do get to Ireland, I worry that you'll find yourself committed to a hospital.

"But here's what I'm willing to do for you. I'll get some maps and travel books for you. I know you love Ireland and miss your mother. Instead of listening, reading, and praying each week, we can explore Ireland and talk about your mother.

"You know, I'd be thrilled if you could actually take this trip and return home safely. When that happens I'll know God has answered our prayers and worked a miracle of healing in your life.

"If you do decide to take the trip, I have no authority to stop you. But your doctor has the authority to stop you if he believes the trip would put you and others in danger. Danny, promise me that you'll discuss it with your doctor. I'll give you my approval when you secure permission from your doctor. Okay?"

"Okay, Daddy O. We have a plan. We have a plan."

****

"Danny! Danny! Oh, there you are? I know I'm a few minutes early. I stopped at Dayton's and your boots were waiting. And here are the two sweaters you wanted.

"Danny, you look awful. Are you sick? It looks like you've lost another five pounds. If you keep losing weight, we'll need to exchange your jeans again."

"Ireland, O Ireland. Ireland, O Ireland. Daddy O, you're here. I don't get hungry anymore. I'm so excited. I'm so excited!

"Yes, I've shed a few more pounds. I don't have any appetite. Sometimes I vomit everything when I try to eat. I can't sleep. Just think, a few more weeks and mother and I will be walking the hills of the Emerald Isle.

"Don't start scolding. Dr. Abuzahab and I argued for fifty minutes. He doesn't approve. But he can't stop me from going. As long as I take my medications, he has no legal grounds for commitment or an emergency hold.

"Thank you, Daddy O, for dreaming with me. I've made my decision. I've made reservations. We've been dreaming and planning for three months. Now it's time to act. I faced the challenge and made a decision.

"Those were good times, Daddy O. We spent three weeks exploring Dublin, more than two weeks reading about Howth's rocky brow, the headland of Dalkey, the broad valley of the Rifer Liffey, the Wicklow Hills, the Golden Vale on the River Shannon, and Limerick. We avoided Belfast—too much smoke.

"I have a printout of my final itinerary. I spend a fortnight near Dublin. I celebrate St. Patrick's Day in his Cathedral listening to memorial prayers and sacred choirs. I'll walk the Wicklow mountain route and the Barrow navigation. Then I'll hike the Tain, Royal Canal, Grand, and Slieve Bloom ways. Let me remind you that 270,000 people walk these trails every year.

"Look, I have in my hand the completed papers. I have them right here. Right in my hand. See for yourself."

"Danny, how did you ever make these arrangements? You have the schedule... bed and breakfast near the Royal Canal...bus passes... even airline tickets. And how did you ever get this credit card? I'm impressed. You managed to make these preparations by phone and have them sent here to your apartment? It's incredible! Congratulations! I certainly underestimated you.

"What's wrong, Danny? Why the tears? I thought you'd be celebrating."

"Look at this memo. Listen to the response from the passport office: 'Birth certificate, two photos, and a personal appearance.' Two photos and a personal appearance, two photos and a personal appearance, two photos and a personal appearance. I can't and I won't. Daddy O, I can't and I won't. I can't and I won't. I've called them repeatedly. No exceptions. I must have two photos and present myself with birth certificate and I D. All these months of praying, dreaming, and planning, of following the call of God and mother, are to no avail. I spent all this money for these tickets. They're non-refundable. What a waste."

"Danny, don't give up now. You can do it. I'll make an appointment at Foto-Fast, take you there in my car, and go with you for the passport interview. This won't be any more frightening than your visits to the doctor's office. Just keep thinking, ' I'm making my regular trip to the doctor.' I'll be right beside you every moment."

"Thank you, Daddy O! Thank you! Thank you. Thank you. I must. I can. I will. Maybe, if you pray with me every step, God will get me to the promised land."

DANNY BOY DEPARTS

"Daddy O, you're here! Come in. Come in. Do come in. See, I'm all packed. Ireland, O Ireland. Ireland, O Ireland, the Emerald Isle. Two days from now, I'll be celebrating in St. Patrick's Cathedral. Next week, I'll be hiking in the Wicklow Mountains.

"I'm exhausted, but I am signed, sealed, stamped. It's been a great experience except for the day we took the pictures. Thank you for praying and walking with me through the long blocks, high stairs, slow lines, and piles of papers."

"You did very well, Danny.

"I came over to tell you goodbye. I'd like to be here when you leave in the morning, but you've made it clear that you have to do this on your own, and I want to respect your wishes. Is there anything else I can do to help you?"

"Thank you, Daddy O! You've have been a wonderful friend. God commissioned you to be my guardian angel. Daddy O, you were dispatched from the throne of God.

"Observe, Daddy O. I have my Bible displayed on my altar of prayer. I contemplate spending my last hours here on my knees, listening to John McCormack, reading the Psalms, and conversing with God and mother. I'll stage a prayer vigil here on my knees until the zero hour. I'm stacking my bags in the hall and leaving the door ajar. If I oversleep, the cab driver will awaken me. I can't sleep. I won't sleep. I don't want to sleep. But I don't dare sleep through zero hour. Zero hour, zero hour, zero hour, my zero hour stands before me. Ireland, O Ireland. Mother, O mother. Thank you, God. Thank you, Daddy O.

"I do have a last request. Before we part, I have a gift from my heart, a gift from my heart. My treasure to a treasured friend, my greatest treasure to you, my greatest friend.

"Contesse my love, Contesse my love, Conesse my love, I am taking you from your wall, your pedestal, your throne, and placing you in the arms of my Daddy O. My love, my love, my love, I am giving you to Daddy O.

"Daddy O, I give you my love. I give you my beloved Contesse."

"Danny, Contesse is yours. She's been yours all of these years. Her home is right here. You'll miss her, but she'll be here waiting for you. I'm going to check your place every few days. We'll both wait patiently for your return."

"No, no, no, Daddy O. I cannot allow Contesse to remain alone. You must receive Contesse as my gift or I cannot go. I won't go. I can't, unless you pledge to care for her. Don't you admire her? Focus on her face. Peer into her eyes. Caress her cheeks. How beautiful, Contesse my love. I could never abandon you, never, never."

"Danny, let's make a contract. I'll take Contesse with me. I promise to place her lovingly on the wall of my office. She'll stay in my home until you return. I'll treasure her while you're gone, but when you return she'll greet you from her throne. See, Contesse is smiling. She approves. Contesse and I will see you on March thirtieth. Together, we'll celebrate your return."

****

March 15

My Dear Daddy O,

It is eleven fifteen. At midnight I leave this world and meet my mother in the Emerald Isle.

I appreciate your friendship. God commissioned you as my comforter, to walk with me through my year of journey. God beckoned me to heaven and home, but I could not prepare for the end alone. You satisfied my longing desire. You inspired me to walk each step.

Forgive my conspiracy. God told me you would understand. I know you would have intervened if I had dared to share my secret scheme. I am sorry for living a lie, but I feel pride in the dramatic way I played my part.

Contesse has found a safe home in your arms and heart. I labeled each book and album with your name. They are my collective gift to you.

I affixed your name to my prayer desk. God and I and Mother plan to visit you at my little altar each day.

Please do not become angry or sad. God decreed my instructions. He predestined my excursion to Emerald Isle, my home. He instructed me to solicit your assistance.

The excitement is ecstatic. I know this is God's ordained plan for me.

In a few minutes I ingest my one hundred hoarded sleep capsules. I loaded father's little revolver and will use it, if I should awaken. I have placed them both on my Bible. I will be discovered kneeling and resting at my place of prayer.

I will share your memory with Mother and God.

Goodbye, until we meet together on the Emerald Isle.

Danny

FATHER'S VOICE

Zella's Story

Touched by the Holy Spirit of God

I was living in darkness,
Living in a world that had no meaning
And I was so hurt inside.
I was full of frustration.
I began walking along the street
  trying to clear my thoughts.
I was wandering as though I was
  searching for an answer.
As I was thinking, I could hear
  the Lord's voice.
He comforted me, holding me
  in his arms.
I was a lost soul needing support.
I cried out, wanting the salvation
  of the Lord.
I felt weak. While my body fainted,
God touched me with the grace
  of his glory.
I became a child of God, witnessing

the works of the Lord.
What was old in me became new
as the Lord lifted me up where I belong.
And that is with him in the glory
of his kingdom.
I remember the day when God
came into my life.
Everything was going wrong
And the living in this world
was not enough to live for.
Oh, how I cried to him
As the darkness became holy
And I saw the spirit of the Lord
reaching out to give me a message.
He said, "Come unto me
And you shall find the inner peace
within yourself.
You are the child of God,
A servant of the Lord,
And I live in souls that
believe in me,
For I am the eternal Lord
And my love for you is beyond itself."
I worshipped him
And I praised his name.
I was touched by the Holy Spirit,

And cleansed with his blessing.
And I know that I was born again
And that God lives on eternally.

I sing this song today in celebration. Twenty years ago I wrote this poem and sang it in the Elliot Park Fellowship. It told my story then. It tells my story now.

I was living in darkness...living in a world that had no meaning. In my searching I wandered into this praying group of spiritual friends. I was able to hear God's voice again. He comforted me... held me...supported me...and touched me.

I remember those dark days. "Everything was going wrong and living in this world was not enough to live for." In despair I tried to kill myself.

Now I live in Ascension Place, a fine group home. It is a beautiful place. My handicapped son Charles, now 23 years of age, lives in Mendota Heights as part of the Dakota Community Program. He is still wheelchair bound and unable to talk.

I work four hours a day as an office assistant in the Spectrum Treatment Center. Dee, my very special friend, lives in the care home with me.

I still hear voices, but the Haldol keeps them under control. Dr. Werner tells me they will go away as I get older, but I will always need medication.

Twenty years ago, God touched me with his grace and what was old in me became new as the Lord lifted me up where I belong.

My first memories as a little girl include going with my mother, father, and eleven brothers and sisters to St. Peter's African Methodist Church on Forty-first Street. We never missed a Sunday. I loved singing in the choir. I was a born-again, baptized, confirmed, and excited member of that little church. I planned on being a Christian for life.

I never lacked girlfriends or boyfriends. I was truly black and beautiful as a teenager. I was smart, made good grades, and had my pick of secretary jobs after graduation. I lived at home, made good money, and spent everything on beautiful clothes.

I fell in love with a cool man. He led me into the drug world and refused to marry me when I became pregnant with his son.

I loved my baby boy, Charles, with all of my heart. He became the joy of my life.

Until this time, I had my problems but I enjoyed living. Everyone seemed to admire my looks and respond to my personality. I felt God was good to me.

My life fell apart when I entered my twenty-fourth year.

My adorable child, my son that I loved more than life, wasn't right. After months of tests the doctors diagnosed him as mentally retarded. His brain refused to grow. They told me that my dear Charles would never walk, or talk, or be able to take care of his personal needs.

My father ordered, "Zella, you have to give Charles up." He wanted me to place him in an institution. We had some terrible arguments. I moved out, got my own apartment, and promised God I would take care of my son on my own.

During this time, I started hearing whispers, like two people talking in low tones in the back of the room. I watched the people around me. I was certain someone was talking about my son and me. I soon realized that the strange talk existed even when I was alone. I decided it came from my own brain.

Over the next weeks and months the voices became loud and wild. I started seeing people that others didn't see. I couldn't make them stop. They took control. Strange words came out of my co-workers' mouths. I asked my supervisor to repeat instructions because I couldn't hear her words over the sounds in my head. I found myself staring into space for minutes at a time. I couldn't do my work.

I knew the words were coming from the Devil, but I couldn't stop from doing what he said. When God talked to me, he told me to do strange and terrible things.

I fought with the voices during the day and they kept me awake each night. I quit going to work. I didn't dare tell anyone what was going on in my life because I believed the Devil possessed my soul.

One Sunday evening I became desperate. I took Charles in his stroller and went to Christ's church on Lake Street. Pastor James asked those who needed God to come forward. I rushed to his side. He put his hand on my forehead and began to pray. The power of God made me fall backward to the floor and pass out.

I awoke to a circle of praying people. The pastor told me that I had been delivered from the power of Satan and God had healed my body. But the voices still rang in my head as I rolled Charles along the sidewalk toward home. God did touch me, but his touch didn't deliver me from the mocking messages of Satan.

Charles grew heavier every day. I didn't have the strength to lift him. If I couldn't take care of my son, Social Services would take him away. I couldn't abandon the one I loved.

God told me the only answer was to kill myself. It would heal the pain of giving up Charles and it would stop the voices. God said, "Come home to me."

I went into the bathroom, opened a new bottle of sleeping pills and ate them all.

I didn't die, but my life did. During the three weeks in the hospital, I lost my faith, my son, my home, my job, my friends, and the respect of my family. In addition, the Haldol medication puffed my pretty face and lovely body into a bloated monster. I had failed God, failed my son, and ruined myself.

I knew I didn't dare listen to the voices anymore. I was afraid God would speak to me again. Talking with Dr. Werner convinced me that all the voices were bad. Gayl, the social worker, released me to the Pleasant Avenue Halfway House after the meds had reduced the voices to a dull roar in the back of my head.

I began an existence in a strange new world of social security disability, Hennepin County Social Services, and a weekly four-hour visit with Charles.

Shari lived in a room down the hall. She invited me to go with her on Sunday morning to the Fair Oaks Fellowship.

I liked the singing. I collected the poems I had written over the years, brought them with me, and read them to the group during the sharing times. I shared my problems and my new friends prayed with me.

The people in the fellowship helped me to know the difference between the voices of my schizophrenia and the messages from God. On Good Friday, 1983, God inspired me with my song "Touched By The Holy Spirit of God." I sang it during our Easter celebration.

I sang from my soul:

Oh, how I cried to him
as the darkness became holy.
And I could see the spirit of the Lord
reaching out to give me a message.
He said, "Come to me
And you shall find the inner peace
within yourself.

OUR LOST BABY

Gertrude's Story

Hi Delta, gu tu see yu. We cudn come las two weeks. We had tu save da money for dis spezul day."

"Oh, this is the day, isn't it? I almost forgot. Why don't you sit here, Bennie, would you like a booth? How about it, Gertrude, is this OK with you?"

"Delta, we need big boot cuz maybe yu and Jean can join like las yu. Member, yu member—yu sit with us for da spezul day?"

"All right.... how about over here? Hardly anyone seems to be stopping today. Look at this place—only three tables taken. The bus from Duluth looked full, but not a single person came in—not even for a cup of coffee. Take the big booth. This is the special day. The biggest day of the year, right?"

"Yu bet dat's right! It's mos portan day to us.... mos portan day dere is fur me an Bennie. Delta, yu nice tu us. Tank you! Tank you!"

"Bennie, you haven't said a word. Aren't you excited, too?"

"Well, it's a sad day, too, you know. Each year I think we'll find out more... or hear from someone. Gertrude talked to the social worker. No news yet. I guess I wonder if we'll ever know."

"Well, Bennie, she did get da papers. She has da papers now. We didn have da papers las yur. Now got papers. Now we got da papers, Delta. Did yu hear dat?"

"Here's your coffee. What do you mean by papers, Gertrude?"

"Yu know, da paper...Da paper which says we can get da records from da hospital... from da school... even see she could 'ave die."

"What do you guys want to eat today? This day Jean can fix you anything you want. CAN'T YOU, JEAN? TODAY IT'S ANYTHING BENNIE AND GERTRUDE WANT, RIGHT???"

"IF YOU SAY SO, DELTA...FIND OUT WHAT THEY WANT...WE'LL DO OUR BEST. WE DON'T HAVE ANY CAVIAR LEFT!"

"Wha dat cavyar, Delta? Wha dat cavyar?"

"Gertrude, caviar is fancy fish eggs. One order would cost more that your monthly allowance. Anyway, depot coffee shops don't serve caviar. Jean's just making fun of me like she sometimes does. So what do you guys want? We can even fix a dinner if you want. It's not on the lunch menu---but today we can make it."

"I want meatloaf. It's my favorite. Gertrude can't have any, though. Beverly says she can't. She didn't lose any weight last week. She can only have a salad."

"Don lis'n to Bennie, Delta. Don lis'n to 'im. I save all my money for dis day... the spezul day. We cel'brate today. How can it be cel'brate with juz salad? Huh, how can dat be cel'brate? I want meatloaf, too."

"So you both want a meatloaf dinner, then? Who's Beverly anyway?"

"She's da sosul worker. Two meatloafs. Let cel'brate begin. I'm gon ta eat da cake too. We brot da cake. A big cake. We can all have da big... big piece."

"OK, two meatloaves---JEAN...TWO MEATLOAVES...SPECIAL FOR BENNIE AND GERTRUDE TODAY."

"Bennie, help me. I can' get da cake out da box."

"You hold the box, honey, while I lift it out. Oh, it's a beauty. It's beautiful. This is even better than last year. The smiling face looks nice. I like it, Gertrude. I really like it."

"Bennie, here da can'les. One box me an one box yu. How much in each box, Bennie? Is dere nuff fur dis day?"

"Twelve in each box...that's exactly right. Two boxes and twenty-four candles."

"How can we get all da can'les on da cake? Bennie, ders too many can'les, da cake too small."

"Don't cry, honey. Gertrude, listen, why are you crying? It'll be a nice cake. Don't cry.

"You know, Bennie, I alays cry. I alays cry. I jus cry da lil while. I don cry like I did dat day in Fare-Bo Home. Tree hul days I cry. Tree hul days. Da nurse she cry. Evrybodee cry. You know what da Chap'n say, I cry cuz it hurz an it hurz cuz I wuv. I wuv so much. I wuv Charlotte so much. I wuv Bennie so much. I wuv for 24 lon yurs...24 lon yurs. Maybe dis yur. We got da papers. Maybe dis yur."

"Don't get yourself all worked up, honey, it's been a long time."

"Bennie, don say dat. Yes'day, member, we pray. We all pray. Our pasta say God can do tings like dat. God do meercles. He do dat."

"Well, you got to stop crying, Gertrude. Let Beverly work on the papers. We're going to celebrate. I'm all done with my candles. Now you do yours, OK?"

"Bennie, one of da can'le broke. Da can'le broke. Not nuff. JEANIE, DO YOU HAVE CAN'LE OUT DERE? JUS ONE CAN'LE?"

"NO, GERTRUDE, WE DON'T HAVE ANY CANDLES. LET BENNIE FIX IT. DELTA'S COMING. MAYBE SHE CAN HELP YOU."

"Here's your dinners, you guys. Two meatloaf dinners with mashed potatoes just for you. Jeanie says you can have all the ice cream you want when you're ready for the cake. Let us know when you're ready. We want to join the party. Oh, here comes James!

"HI JAMES! BUSY TODAY?"

"Good morning, Delta. Well, spring break you know. The college kids with all their boxes...Hellooooo, Gertie."

"DON CALL ME GERTIE! JAMES, YU DON CALL ME GERTIE. I HAY GERTIE. NEBER, NEBER, NEBER CALL ME GERTIE. FOR LEBEN YURS EBRY BODY CALL ME GERTIE. EBRY BODY—NURSE ELLA, MR. PALEU, EBRY BODY IN FARE-BO CALL ME GERTIE, GERTIE, GERTIE. AN ALL DA UDDURS, WHEN CHARLOTTE WAS IN MY TUMMY, DE CALL ME DIRTY GERTIE, DIRTY GERTIE, DIRTY GERTIE. JAMES, YU STOP DAT. YU NEBER CALL ME GERTIE!"

"I like Gertie. That's a cute name. It's sure a lot better than Gerrrr-trude."

"James, you quit it. You leave her alone. Please, just leave us alone."

"OK, Bennie, have it your way, I'll have coffee with Delta. At least she likes me."

"Gertrude, honey, this is good. You aren't eating at all. You said you were so hungry. No diet today, you said, and now you aren't eating. Come on. Eat. Come on. Let's celebrate."

"I member too mush, Bennie, I member too mush. Yu tole me we wuz jus like man and wife. Das what yu say. But Mr. Paleu, he yells, 'Yu are not man an wife. Yu neber be man an wife in dis home...neber...neber...neber.' I don forget dat. I don forget dat.

"Den dey took Charlotte.

"Den da guvnur change de law and make us leave Fair-Bo. Firs dey won let us leave and take Charlotte. Den, later, dey tell us tu leave da home. Why Bennie, Why??"

"We were happy to leave, honey. Don't forget that. When the nurse said we could leave the Faribault Home and go on our own, we were happy. You were happy. We all were happy. We did OK, Gertrude. Remember, Beverly told us that we proved it was the right thing. We did it."

"I tink it too har, Bennie. Too har. All our money goes to Lou fur room and eats. We save, save, save but we neber hav nuttin."

"We have enough for today, honey. It's time for the cake. Let's light the candles. DELTA, JEANIE, WE'RE READY FOR THE CAKE. I'M LIGHTING THE CANDLES. TIME TO SING!"

"'WE'RE COMING, BENNIE. ED WILL TAKE OVER FOR JEANIE. LIGHT THE CANDLES!"

"Lead da song Delta. Lead da song."

"Wait, Gertrude, I'm going to lead us in a toast—a real toast. Jeanie brought some cherry coke and real glasses. We are going to do this right. TO CHARLOTTE, FOR TWENTY-FOUR HAPPY YEARS, WHEREVER YOU ARE. WE WISH YOU TWENTY-FOUR MORE HAPPY YEARS. WE LOVE YOU."

"Excuse me! Excuse me! Please excuse me. Did you say your name was Bennie? Bennie, right? And this is Gertrude? I've been sitting here three tables away, listening, and I can't wait any longer."

"Yes, my name is Bennie. Who are you? What's wrong? Why are you crying? What do you want from us?"

"My name is Charlotte. I heard every word. I heard you say you had a daughter born at the "Faribault Home For The Retarded" twenty-four years ago today. Listen.... listen... I'm sorry, I can hardly talk, but I know I was born in that home twenty-four years ago today. Could you be my Dad and Mom? It couldn't be, could it? COULD YOU BE MY DAD AND MOM? I THINK YOU'RE MY MOM AND DAD!"

Five weeks later, the social worker found papers verifying Charlotte as the daughter of Bennie and Gertrude, ending the twenty-four-year search of the parents.

Bennie and Gertrude still live independently in a small south Minneapolis apartment. Each year, the three-member family continues the tradition of holding a daylong celebration on Charlotte's birthday.

DADDY DO YOU LOVE ME?

Donna's Story

MAMA AND GOD

Mama told me I could go with them to town and eat hot beef sandwiches at the old cafe. Then, after we got back home and the chores were done, we could go to the dance. I loved to dance. I wanted to watch the young farm couples laugh and drink and flirt to the sounds of music at the Old Legion Hall.

"Mama, could I wear lipstick just this once on this special fun day?" I asked. I knew that eleven-year-old girls were way too young. My heart jumped inside when I heard her say, "Yes, Donna Lou, if that will make you happy, you may wear it this once."

On our way home from town with my tummy full of mashed potatoes and beef gravy, everything in my life changed.

Mama, Daddy, and Olive Mae rode in the front seat. Everett sat in the middle of the back seat between my nine-year-old brother, Dwayne, and me. Mama called out, "I don't think that car is going to stop." I could see it slowly coming down the dirt road to the Highway 12 corner.

"I'm sure it will," my Daddy said. Then his voice turned into a scream, "It's not stopping.... It's not stopping."

Our car turned over and over, forever and ever.

Suddenly, everything became quiet. Dust and smoke choked my throat and hurt my eyes. Someone reached in, pulled me through the window, and then dragged out my brother.

Olive Mae yelled, "Laura is under the car!" I saw Mama crushed into the ground. Everett kept trying to lift the wrecked door. Daddy was pulling on Mama's shoulder.

Then Daddy held her in his arms. She looked like a dirty rag doll. Nobody said anything for a long time. I could hear the siren like a baby crying far, far away.

Daddy said, "I can't wait any longer." He jumped up with Mama and ran down the road toward the flashing light. He lifted her in the back door and climbed in. The ambulance took off for the hospital.

Everett, Olive Mae, and Dwayne followed a neighbor into her house. I walked along behind them. I passed a woman standing alone in the ditch. She had been driving the car that hit us.

I knew Mama was dead. No one told me, but I heard them talking.

After hours of waiting, Everett and Olive Mae took me with them to their house. I guess my brother went home with Daddy. Olive Mae put me in her bed and told me to go to sleep.

I remember the funeral. They brought Mama into the living room of our house. Olive Mae said, "It's all right to touch her," but I couldn't. Her face looked pretty. It hurt me to look at the purple swelling around her neck.

She stayed there all night. Many people came to look at her. In the morning two men in black suits took the casket away. We followed them down the road past the school to the old Powell Presbyterian Church.

The black hearse carried her to the little graveyard on our road to town.

That summer they put a big gray stone on the grave. I still see the words: "Laura Riley Hodson ... 1908-1942."

I remember Olive Mae and Everett coming to live in our house with Daddy, Dwayne, and me.

Daddy hardly ever talked to me after that. He looked terribly sad. He sat alone in the living room and said, again and again, "Why didn't I fix that car door? Maybe Laura would still be here." I knew the lock on the door was broken. One time, as we went around the corner, it fell open and dumped me out on the dusty road.

I remember not having any good clothes to wear and holes in my shoes. The cactus stickers got me when I walked after the cows.

Mama used to make me cute outfits. One time she made me a little white seersucker dress. She said, "You look just like Shirley Temple." She sent me out to the barn to show Daddy. He didn't say anything, but I thought it was darling.

I wondered why Daddy and Olive Mae didn't care how I dressed.

But one day, after school, as I burst into the kitchen, I saw a new pair of brown shoes sitting on top of the frig. I thought, "Dwayne has a new pair of shoes." Olive Mae handed them to me and asked me to try them on. She said, "They're yours." I hugged them. It felt so good.

And the day I turned twelve, I dashed into the living room, threw my coat on the couch, and ran to the kitchen. Olive Mae said, "Go back in there and see what your Daddy got you."

Against the wall stood a gorgeous piano, just my size. I touched the keys. Daddy watched me from the kitchen. I thought, "He must have noticed me trying to play every piano I could find." He smiled like he was surprised as I slowly banged out "The Tennessee Waltz."

Daddy walked into the room, came to my side, and said, "I got it for you. I want you to learn how to play and sing."

I remember telling Aunt Lucy, "I prayed that God would take Mama to heaven." She said, "You can't pray for her now. She either made it to heaven or it's too late." Aunt Lucy started crying and told me, "Last summer, Laura said to me, 'Lucy, I will be a Christian if you will.' I said, 'No. If your mother missed heaven, it's all my fault.'"

I remember the long days. They seemed dark, like there was no sun. Grown-ups came to our house to talk with Daddy, Everett, and Olive Mae about Mama's accident, but they didn't want me to hear them. They whispered and spoke in low tones. When I came close, they would stop and wait for me to go away. Most of the time they treated me like I wasn't there.

I remember the one person who talked to me about Mama. I was hiding in the corner of the kitchen by the cupboard with tears running down my face. My best friend, Betty Lou, found me. She knelt down, put her arm around my neck, and hugged me.

She said, "I'm sorry."

DADDY AND GOD

I didn't want Daddy to leave me alone. Why did they have to die, first Mama and now my Daddy? We went to the hospital every day after school, before going home to do the chores.

One time Quin, a farmer friend who lived down the road, put a box of chocolates on the bed stand. Daddy felt very hungry and decided to try eating one small piece. It made the cancer in his stomach hurt terrible. He started screaming and we had to leave. Only Dorothy, Daddy's new girlfriend could stay. "Why her?" I wondered. It made me mad.

One afternoon Daddy welcomed us with the biggest grin. Since Mama died, he had always looked very sad. Today, he couldn't seem to stop smiling.

Lucy said, "Doesn't he look radiant?" I didn't really know what radiant meant, but it made me feel like laughing to see him happy. He looked right at me. He asked me to come to him. He put his arm around me and told me, "Pastor Leigh came to see me today. We prayed. God loves me. God forgives me. I'm going to Heaven."

He pointed to Dorothy, seated in the chair by the window. She looked like she had been crying. "She's been reading the Bible to me, but we won't be together as man and woman again."

I couldn't stop looking at his happy face.

On Mother's Day, Daddy asked Dwayne and me to come into his room alone. He wanted to talk to us.

He asked us to stand close to his side. "Don't marry just any Tom, Dick, or Harry," he said to me.

He told Dwayne and me, "Say your prayers before you go to bed each night."

I promised, "I will Daddy."

"Your Aunt Lucy became a Christian, too, after your mama died. That's why I want her to be your guardian. She'll take care of you and there will be enough money for both of you to go to college."

He asked me to lean down. He kissed me for the first time in my life.

I thought, "Oh no! Daddy will never hear me play the piano or sing!"

That week Daddy died. The hospital called out to the farm. Olive Mae announced it to all of us sitting around the kitchen table.

Pastor Leigh preached the funeral at the Powell Church. The obituary in the funeral folder read, "After his remarkable conversion to Christ in St. Luke's Hospital, Delbert Hodson became a member of the Ipswich Wesleyan Methodist Church with full membership." The Pastor said, "In a dream, while in the hospital, Delbert saw his wife, Laura, in heaven, walking in a beautiful rose garden. He is with her now."

Three women sang in the service. One broke down and cried when she looked at us kids on the front row. She couldn't finish the song.

After the funeral, I went to my room, knelt down by the bed and prayed, "God, please show me how to get to Heaven."

LUCY AND GOD

I worshiped my Aunt Lucy. My eyes saw her as the most beautiful woman in the world. Tall and slender, with dark-tanned skin, she reminded me of a queen. An artist, she built a beautiful home surrounded by acres of rocks, flowers, and rose gardens. Her long fingers made fine woodcarvings and painted beautiful nature pictures on the inside walls of her house.

She lived on Lake Mitchell with her second husband, the manager of Home Furniture Company. Compared to all of my farm relatives, she seemed worldly and wealthy.

Lucy had loved Mama as her favorite of the four sisters. When she got killed, Lucy cried for three weeks. All day long she repeated the same words like a prayer, "Jesus, save me... save me... save me."

"One day everything changed. God saved me. He gave me salvation."

"What do you mean by saved?" I asked.

"God filled me with love. A love so wonderful I can't explain it. It felt so strong—like I couldn't take any more. It's unbelievable. It's like a miracle. After all these years of having nothing to do with God, I know I'm a Christian and I'm going to church."

I didn't know what to think. Everett and Olive Mae laughed. They didn't have time for what they called "that religious stuff."

After I graduated from the eighth grade, Aunt Lucy told me, "Come live with me this summer. In the fall I'll send you to boarding school." I left all my clothes and things in my old room at our farm. Aunt Ella helped Lucy alter my mother's dresses for me to wear. "Still like new. They'll last you a long time."

My insides cried, "You can't make me wear these. I feel like an old woman." Ella put her hand on my cheek. "It's all we have and you'll look very nice." I put one on. What else could I do?

Everything seemed strange and wrong after that. Daddy had owned the farm, which meant it belonged to Dwayne and me, but my uncle Everett got to run the farm, and we had to leave. My little brother put his two pairs of ragged underwear in a paper sack and walked across the field to Uncle Melvin's place, and I got in the car with Aunt Lucy.

Soon after I came to her place, Lucy asked me to go with her to some "special meetings" at the Wesleyan church. She said, "I'm terribly busy and I don't have the time, but I think we should go."

I had never gone to church. I knew Lucy didn't believe in lipstick, so I rubbed mine off and I didn't wear any that night.

I don't know what the preacher said, but at the end he asked, "Is there anyone who would like to come forward, kneel at the altar and pray?" I wanted to go, no question. I felt God wanted me to come to him. Lucy prayed with me, asked a few questions, and announced, "Well, you're saved. You don't need to pray anymore. You can go."

The next day I felt free and happy. I thought, "Now I'm a Christian and someday I'll see Mama and Daddy in heaven."

Lucy told me all the things I needed to do if I wanted to be a Christian. I couldn't wear jewelry or make-up anymore. I needed to stop curling my hair. And "Christians never go to the picture shows or dances." I didn't want to stop dancing, but I felt I had to in order to be a Christian.

I liked Lucy's place. My cousin Cameron and I went fishing and boating. We swam and played in the lake. But I got the feeling that Lucy wished I didn't live there. Many times she told me, "It costs a lot for you to eat." I said, "Why don't you take money out of Daddy's estate and pay for it?" She said, "I couldn't do that. Laura would turn over in her grave."

Cam, Lucy's husband, started coming to my room each night. He watched me get undressed and get into bed. Then he would kiss me good night. It made me feel scared and I told Lucy. She said, "Hmm, I'll fix that." He never bothered me again.

After that, she began pushing me away. "Please leave me alone. All I want is a little peace and quiet."

She didn't like my breasts. She said, "They're so big." When I started bleeding soon after my tenth birthday, Mama told me, "I expected it because you look so developed." I wanted to be little and flat like Lucy.

Lucy felt I couldn't do anything right. "Don't you even know how to fry an egg? "Don't squeeze the strawberries. Now you went and ruined them!" "Can't you do anything?" Each time she bawled me out, I whispered under my breath, "If Mama taught me, I don't remember."

At age fourteen, I belonged to no one. Nobody wanted me and I had no place to go. I longed for someone to love me. I felt old and fat wearing Mama's dresses. Nothing I touched was mine. I didn't fit anywhere. Aunt Lucy didn't want me any more. Uncle Everett and Aunt Olive Mae were too busy. Aunt Ella said "I can take Dwayne, he can sleep with the boys, but I have no place for a girl." I saw the boarding school as far away from anyone I knew. It made me feel lonely.

I remember standing in Lucy's house, looking out the window, and saying out loud, "If I were only a boy, I could run away and never come back."

THE CHURCH AND GOD

I lived at the boarding school until I turned eighteen. At school, the church acted as my stern and strict parents. I lived, worked, studied, and survived under the watchful eye of teacher, preceptress, and dean of women.

I arrived at the Wessington Springs Academy with four of Mama's made-over dresses, a bra, one panty, and a pair of shoes. I wondered, "Does the school provide my clothes, too?"

I remember the first night the dorm mother found me, after hours, washing out my underthings. I explained, "I have to do these every night before I go to bed." She exploded at me, "You must have more underwear than that!" I meekly confessed, "But I don't."

Betty Harold worked downtown at Springs Cafe. She said, "I'll get Gene to hire you for two hours each afternoon." He did, and after my first check I sparkled in fresh new underwear. Soon I pranced around, the envy of the other kids, in my own outfits. I told her, "You saved my life." And how!

I entered high school with one dream in mind. I knew I had musical talent and I felt God had called me to sing. So, on the first day of the ninth grade I added my name to the try-out list for the chorus. The second day I reported to the music room, where Mrs. Kline, the department head, asked me to join two girls and sing second soprano. I didn't know what soprano was. I couldn't even open my mouth. I rushed from the building, ran to my room, and threw myself across the bed. I cried through supper and sobbed all night.

I stayed in my room the next day. I just couldn't go back to school.

Miss Vincent asked my roommate, "Where's Donna?"

Shirley replied, "She feels like dying because she can't sing."

During lunch hour, I heard a knock at my door. Mrs. Kline asked, "May I come in?" walked across the room, and sat down on my bed. "Do you want to tell me what happened yesterday?"

My pillow-muffled sounds told Mrs. Kline about my twelfth birthday. "I promised Daddy at his funeral service, 'I will finish college and become a church singer, just like those young women in the trio.'"

Mrs. Kline waited until I washed my eyes and got dressed. She led me to her studio, listened to me sing, and announced, "You have a nice voice. I'll teach you. With enough training, perhaps you'll become one of the vocalists selected for the traveling a cappella choir."

She cared, coached, and kept her promise. She let me call her Kay.

Miss Schamehorn weighed only ninety pounds. The tiny legs, crippled by polio, forced her to walk with crutches. Talent and soul poured through her trained hands whenever they touched the piano keys. Schooled in tough love, she determined I would earn a bachelor's of science in music education with majors in music theory and voice, and a minor in piano. She pushed, pleaded, demanded, and criticized. Her faith reached through my failures and made me believe in myself.

I left college with a music degree, my husband Orin, and our first child, Timothy, in my womb. "God has answered the prayers of my Daddy."

I thought. "Growing up has healed the hurt and pain of those terrible years."

I was still so very young.

ORIN AND GOD

The Bishop called us "church planters." Our job: resurrect dead churches. The alternative: preside over their burial and ours. No one told us how or why.

But on August 16, 1958, my husband, Orin, and my two sons—Timothy, age 5, and Michael, age 4—moved with me into the First Free Methodist Church house in Sioux Falls, South Dakota. There I entered the darkest days of my 27 years.

The builders, eighty years ago, had jammed the home against the railroad tracks. In fact, someone had beveled the southwest corner of the structure to keep it from trespassing on Milwaukee Road property. The regular roaring and shaking of passing trains interrupted each day and ruined our nights.

The house stood oblivious to any attempts to remodel and repair. It had gone too long. Every wall and floor looked crooked. One day Timothy spilled a glass of milk; it ran into the sagging northwest corner of the dining room and dripped through a hole into the basement.

Our two tiny bedrooms were in the attic. To reach the only bathroom, I had to help Michael down the ladder, through the kitchen, down the stairs into the dirt-walled basement, up one huge step to the sink level, and onto a final riser, the stool platform.

Once a man from the General Church office stayed in our bedroom while we slept on the living room couch. I heard him growling to himself as he tried to get his big shoes down the creaking steps, "What a beast of a parsonage!"

We had little money for food and nothing for clothes. The local Board wanted the church closed. The lay leader announced the day we arrived, "We don't have the money to support a pastor" and set out to prove it. Orin insisted we could survive until things turned around, but I knew I would never make it.

One loyal church family kept us supplied with groceries, but each week I faced the challenge of finding change for the laundromat. Meanwhile, the few church members lived in beautiful homes, drove late model cars, and paraded around in new outfits.

Each morning I dragged myself out of bed, fixed breakfast for the boys, piled toys in the middle of the ragged living room rug, and crawled on the couch. I wanted to sleep and never wake up.

Painful dreams began disturbing my sleep. My screams, crying out for my Daddy, kept Orin awake at night.

I remember climbing those rickety attic stairs, wiping the tears from my eyes and beating each step with my fist.

I had given my life to the church and she had abandoned me, just like everyone else. My soul screamed, "How can God, and Orin, and the church make me exist like this?"

My skin felt damp from the daily fog of sadness. My faced burned with the fire of anger. I fought to keep from drowning.

On June 21 of our first year, about seven in the evening, the phone rang. A church couple wanted someone to help them deal with a marital problem. Orin agreed to meet them at their place.

I begged, "Please tell them no. Don't go. You can't leave me." I never wanted Orin to go away, especially in the evening. In my most powerful secret fantasy, I pictured myself going into his study where he would see me, drop everything, pick me up in his arms, and carry me off to bed. The church always came first. I, often, wondered why he hadn't taken the vow of celibacy.

He said, "I do have to go. Will you pray for me while I'm gone?" I heard my voice say, "Yes, I will." After he left, I knelt down by a red vinyl kitchen chair.

Suddenly an all-consuming, overwhelming power filled me. Waves and waves of pure love flowed through my mind and trembled through every muscle of my body.

I knew in that instant that God loved me unconditionally.

I wanted that love to keep flowing through my body. My thoughts prayed the line from an old hymn: "Sweep over my spirit forever, I pray, in fathomless billows of love."

I found myself outdoors, walking up and down the sidewalk in front of that old house and singing the great hymns: "How Great Thou Art" and "The Love of God" but these words didn't begin to explain the greatness of God's love.

My mind pictured a huge green and blue world spinning in the sky. A new church, under construction, suddenly appeared on the globe. Orin stood on the roof of the building in his black clergy suit. God said, "See, this is Orin, the first person who ever loved you. I sent him into your life to give you love."

Then I saw the church congregation seated in their pews. The voice from heaven announced, "I have given you all of these people to love."

I walked in the house and down the stairs to the old bathroom mirror. My face beamed with happiness. I looked again and again. I couldn't stop smiling.

A shivering took over my body. I put on my coat, wondering why I felt cold on such a warm evening.

Orin returned home to find me pacing through the house, repeating, "Everything is so beautiful." He told me later, "You went to the picture hanging on the wall, ran a finger over its surface, and repeated, 'Isn't it beautiful? Everything looks beautiful!'"

I stepped out of my dark, fear-filled cage into a bright and beautiful world.

Before the year ended, I went back to college, completed an internship, and received my teaching license.

The following Christmas, I thrilled to a standing ovation as Principal Songstad congratulated my ninety-voice school choir and me.

Through songs of joy I thanked God for his great love.

MICHAEL AND GOD

On November 5, 1952, Timothy came bouncing into our world.

I saw him as the answer to every mother's dream. His cute dimples, spontaneous smile, and love for strangers made him the darling of the Mother's Club. He filled all my inner longings. I gave him my heart.

Eight months later, unplanned and without any warning, the doctor told me, "Let's set the due date for March 10, 1954." On that day, Michael Dwayne came into my life, right on schedule.

The two babies seemed to belong in different worlds. Timothy received attention from everyone and me. Michael spent hours in the crib without a sound.

At four years of age Timothy invaded every space in our home, while Michael, with his shy smile, sat on the sidelines, sucking his thumb.

Timothy turned sixteen as a bright, assertive, leader and a friend of everyone.

Michael turned fourteen as an intelligent, sensitive, artistic and shy introvert.

Orin criticized Michael daily. Michael responded with anger. Arguments followed. Life became a continual round of yelling conflicts.

Michael's explanation was, "I don't disrespect. I simply express my feelings."

One evening, while reading a book, alone in my bed, a voice spoke to me. God told me these exact words: "The reason Michael is that way is because of your lack of love for him."

I told Orin, "I know what God wants us to do: just love Michael more, accept him as a beautiful person, and never criticize him again." That hour we determined to change.

That day Michael began to change.

On Saturday, eleven weeks later, Michael came home about noon, went immediately to his room, and closed and locked the door. I wondered why he wanted to be alone, but said nothing. Orin and I needed to go to the church for a leadership meeting and I thought of telling Michael that we would be gone a few hours, but decided not to disturb his privacy.

When we returned three hours later, Michael met us as we walked in the door. He said, "Will you come with me to my room? I want to show you something."

We opened the door to an impressionistic self-portrait of Michael, painted in acrylic, poised on an easel in the center of the room. It pictured his head and hands in a posture of prayer. Clouds of black and blue and brown billowed behind him. A bright light of yellow, orange, and red flowed toward his face.

"Mom, Dad, I want to present this portrait as a gift to you. I want you to know that I love you." He hugged us both.

When we finally moved out of that house, I refused to let the movers touch that painting. I carried it carefully, myself, to our new home.

TIMOTHY AND GOD

On June 10th, I stepped into Hallmark to buy a Father's Day card for Orin's father. I called him Dad and he called me Little Half Pint. He had no daughters of his own. We pretended to love each other and it felt nice, but I still had those lonely times when my heart cried for Daddy. Oh, how I wished he could know his grandsons!

As I stood looking at the display, that familiar warm loving voice of God said to me, "I'll be your father."

At that moment, I let God move into the empty space left in my life when Daddy died.

Suddenly the old pain and struggle stopped. I remembered the words of Jesus when the resurrected Lazarus came out of the tomb, bound in grave clothes: "Loose him and let him go."

I thought, "I'm free. I'm ready." And then I thought, "I want to do something eternal with my life."

That Father's Day I began praying a constant pleading prayer: "Father, make my life worthwhile. My years are half gone and I feel so useless. I need a purpose, a mission, a ministry. Save me from a meaningless existence."

It started to snow the Friday following Christmas. I stood alone in our home, watching the flakes come down. Church headquarters had insisted that Orin lead a family life retreat in Indiana. Timothy and Michael had left earlier in the week for the annual youth Snow Camp near Little Falls.

I found myself standing by the living room fireplace repeating that simple, desperate prayer: "Father, make my life worthwhile."

In that moment, I experienced the same overpowering love that I'd felt that day, ten years ago, in the old parsonage. The fathomless billows of love swept over my spirit.

Suddenly, in my mind, I saw Jerry and Bill, two young men on Timothy's wrestling team, walking toward me across the school gym floor. A warm rush of love made me gasp for air. My ears heard God's voice: "Will you pray for them?" An instant response pushed through my lips: "Father, it would be a privilege."

One evening a few days later, after the regular wrestling workout, Timothy invited Bill and Jerry to our home. I made chocolate chip cookies and served them with Cokes. Jerry thanked me for the cookies. "They remind me of my grandmother. Whenever I visit she makes these. They're my favorite."

Although he was usually quiet, tonight he kept talking. "I stay with my grandparents and work on my uncle's farm in the summer. They always go to church and take me with them. My mom was raised in that country church, but my dad never goes. He owns the Mobil Station and has to run it on Sundays. Besides, he thinks my mom's religion is way out."

The sharing and talking among us continued well into the night.

Afterward, as I listened and silently prayed, I felt joy flow through my mind. I sensed that God had chosen me to participate in the divine and eternal mission of loving and accepting these young people. And I knew that my presence would, somehow, help them find their way in life.

The next night, three other high school classmates came with Tim,

Bill, and Jerry into our home. A few days afterward, friends from outside of the team joined the group. Night after night they would lounge on the living room rug and talk for hours about the war, President Nixon, and the draft.

One night Bill asked me, "What do you think about going to fight in Vietnam?" I told him, "When Timothy asked our church to pray about his decision to become a conscientious objector, Ron, a man in our church, came to me and told me that in this war one couldn't be a Christian and refuse to fight, because we were fighting godless Communism.

"Well, I told him that there was a paragraph in our church manual stating that any member of the church has the right to take a stand against war and claim conscientious objector status. War has divided Christians for centuries. I support Timothy, but I also pray for two of his friends in church who have volunteered to go. They're planning for careers in the armed services."

"Would you remember to pray for me?" Bill asked me.

"Every day."

I wondered why they wanted me to join in their conversation. What attracted them? They seemed drawn together by something.

One day Gary's girlfriend showed up at the door. She started bringing others. For the rest of the school year, five to seven nights a week, my home filled with young people.

Over and over I heard God's voice saying, "Don't tell them what to do. Don't give them any advice. Just love them."

Bobbi came to escape a father who abused her sexually when he found her home alone. In wonder, she said, "I feel such love here, just so much love."

Bill shared his fear of his father, who demanded that he enroll in the Air Force Academy and become a fighter pilot.

Jerry wanted to know how to leave his girlfriend. His mother's religion believed that one act of sex sealed the relationship for life and that breaking up, like divorce, sent people to hell.

Lynn asked for prayer. Her father had attempted suicide in a fit of depression.

Robin searched for help in finding Mr. Right.

Playing, talking, sharing, thinking, crying and listening together, these young people experienced a fellowship of love and faith. They discovered solutions, made decisions, and felt supported.

Listening, accepting and caring, I let God's love for Timothy's friends flow through my life. Each day filled me with excitement and a sense of deep fulfillment.

Four years later, one of those young women, Robin, married my son Michael.

Sharing God's love made my life worthwhile and gave me joy.

DONNA AND GOD

Thirty years had passed since the day Daddy died and abandoned his little girl. Daily, the spiritual healing of God flowed fresh in my soul.

Then, on my forty-first birthday, I suddenly stood on the edge of a swirling, sucking whirlpool of blackness. The District Church Board and my husband, the newly elected superintendent, had decided, without consulting me, to move the regional office to Minneapolis. I would be jerked away from my music profession, my spiritual mission, my friends, my worthwhile life, my joy, and the call of God.

Until now, trusting life had felt like walking on water. Now the waves buckled and swayed beneath by feet. Why? And, how? I couldn't face it.

What could I do? Desperate, I decided to enter into a ten day fast.

On day three, I came home, walked into the music room and let my eyes rest again on the little piano daddy had given me. Then I turned and began to walk through the archway into the living room.

God's voice spoke. It sounded about three feet away and came into my right ear. As I turned, I heard, "If you will do this for me I will give you a garden of roses."

I waited.

Silence.

No clues. No explanation. No understanding.

But I knew God would walk with me through the valley and the shadow. The fear of drowning disappeared and a calming love rippled through my heart.

In June, with the school term over, I went with Orin to visit the Twin Cities. Jim, a pastor from one of the churches, and his wife Laveen had agreed to give me a tour of Minneapolis.

The first words from Jim's mouth were, "Donna, how would you like to see your new home? The board doesn't have possession, but we can drive by and you could see it."

Jim drove us west on Ninetieth Street to Lyndale Avenue and turned north. We stopped for the light at Forty-Sixth Street, drove through Forty-Third and stopped.

"There it is."

I stepped out of the car before a two-story brick and stucco house. A wide curving sidewalk made its way through landscaped shrubs and lawn to the street.

"The huge living room has a fireplace that covers an entire wall, and there are four large bedrooms upstairs."

Jim circled the block to head back and Laveen announced, "And right over there, down Forty-Second Street, is my favorite place in the Twin Cities."

"What's that Laveen?"

"The Rose Garden."

In that moment, I knew that in that unfamiliar house, before the warmth and light of the fireplace, I would find fresh space and soil for the mission of my life.

In August, we moved into our new home. I circled the fireplace with comfortable couches, decorated the guest rooms with wall coverings and prints of blooming roses, and waited expectantly for the promise to unfold.

Willy, one of Timothy's friends, had moved from Sioux Falls to Minneapolis to attend the University of Minnesota. One day in October, he stopped by our house. He wanted to get in touch with Timothy and asked for his college address. As we visited, I shared with him my story of the rose garden house.

The following Saturday, he invited me to go with him and meet two of his lifetime buddies. They had been Eagle Scouts together. Gerry had just returned from Europe after running from the draft. His application for admission to the university had been accepted, but he still faced all of the federal charges. Nick had dropped all plans of college because of alcohol, drug, and disabling health problems.

That day, while riding with these new friends in Nick's old beat-up green pickup, the words of Jesus flashed and focused in my mind: "Go and find out what this scripture means: 'I do not want animal sacrifices, but kindness. For I have not come to call the respectable people, but the outcasts.'"

Soon Gerry, his girlfriend Carol, and Willy were hanging out in our home. Carol began inviting isolated minority students from Hawaii, California, and New Mexico. That trio opened the door of the rose garden house to a growing fellowship of university students and young adults rejected by family, church, or traditional society.

Carol had enrolled in a master's program at the University of Minnesota. She was intelligent, educated, sophisticated, healthy and lost. Carol and her lover Gerry, the draft dodging, war protesting, teen-ager had disappeared from Sioux Falls, South Dakota the week of high school graduation. Months later the authorities located them in Switzerland living in a farmer's barn.

Her parents, a highly-respected Christian Japanese-American couple, had been displaced to the Midwest after World War II. Her father headed the Department of Economics at Sioux Falls College. The parents were hurt and humiliated by Carol's attitude and lifestyle.

Carol became my dear friend.

I remember the day she asked me to invite her parents to travel from Sioux Falls and stay in our home. She felt ready to take the first step in rebuilding relationships.

From that cautious beginning, mother and father and Carol became regular guests at our house. The parents celebrated with us the day Carol was married to Fong Eng by my husband as they stood in our living room. They stayed with us the weekend Carol graduated from the University of Minnesota with a doctorate in educational counseling.

Other visitors to our house were simple prodigals like Kenny. He deliberately chose a lifestyle that separated him from God, his mother, and her church. Then when failures, addictions, and divorce brought him down, his own fears perpetuated his lostness. He simply needed a bridge of acceptance. Our home provided it for him. It helped him turn and begin his journey toward renewal.

Others needed a time and place to grieve over losses and discover the strength to continue living. There was Stephen, who drove to our house from Michigan after being expelled from John Hopkins University and rejected by parents because of his compulsive love affair with a teenage boy. Two weekends of listening, caring, and understanding friends helped him accept both his sexual identity and his parents' attitude.

John knocked on our door at midnight. His first sexual experience with a male had been exciting and frightening. He felt he had to choose. Either he would lose his own self-identity or become an outcast in the eyes of his parents, church, and society. By morning the angry sobbing had stopped. All he needed was one night with supportive and caring friends.

I had no agenda with these people. My focus was fellowship. I told the story of the rose garden house to each new friend, explained where they could find the key to our home, and invited them to share in our weekly Saturday night potluck suppers.

Each relationship felt like a gift. We seldom touched, even to shake hands, and we never hugged. It seemed too sacred. But I had this consciousness of God, in a form like an angel, going to each person, tenderly touching his lips to each temple, and then, in a caress, gently sliding both hands down the cheeks until the tips of the fingers left the person's face. My mind watched this intimate, invisible greeting of love touch each person whenever we came together.

An atmosphere of acceptance and support filled these fellowship times. I never heard an argument. Listening, caring, and supporting words surrounded everyone, including newcomers.

Each day I would meditate on a few words clipped to my Bible from Thomas Merton: *Prophet in the Belly of a Paradox*: "You are probably striving to build an identity in your work... using it to protect against nothingness, annihilation... All the good that you will do will come not from you but from the fact that you have allowed yourself to be used by God's love. The real hope, then, is in God, who is making something good out of it in some way we cannot see."

On early summer mornings, I would walk down to Lyndale Park, sit by the fountain, watch the gentle mist rise from the hundreds of blooming roses, and quietly sing Bette Midler's song:

"When the night has been too lonely
And the road has been too long
And you think that love is only
For the lucky and the strong,
Just remember in the winter,
Far beneath the bitter snow,
Lies the seed that with the sun's love
In the spring becomes the rose."

There, I would pray: "Thank you, God, for finding and loving me. Thank you for finding and loving all these other beautiful people through me. Thank you, God, for our garden of roses."

520509

Made in the USA